"The joy of reading a clearly yourself, and h ing on the topic of wh any Christian in America.

—Justin Whitmel Earley, lawyer, speaker, and author

"*Called to Freedom* is a breath of fresh air. Rooted in biblical wisdom, it accessibly retrieves central Reformation insights for some of the most pressing issues of our day. Littlejohn is a thoughtful Protestant voice on the nature of both spiritual and political liberty."

—Eric Gregory, professor of religion, Princeton University

"Americans love freedom, but many of us embrace profoundly warped understandings of spiritual, moral, and political liberty. *Called to Freedom* offers thoughtful reflections on each of these freedoms and considers how properly understanding them might inform how we think about technology, markets, and religious liberty. Every Christian family should buy a copy of this book, read it together, and discuss its implications."

—Mark David Hall, professor of government, Regent University, and senior fellow, Center for Religion, Culture, and Democracy

"Christians are called to freedom. What might this mean, in light of our understanding that economic, political, and, more recently, technological freedom cannot, by themselves, deliver us from bondage? Brad Littlejohn reminds us that we have been here before, and that the Christian Reformers can again be our guides. Here is a book that understands that freedom can only find its true support in the purified human heart."

—Joshua T. Mitchell, professor of political theory, Georgetown University, and chairman, Common Sense Society

"*Called to Freedom* is a tour de force and a much-needed consideration of freedom as defined by Christianity. Brad Littlejohn's book represents one of the most important books on freedom to emerge in recent decades. This work is informed by Christianity's classical intellectual tradition, and it engages some of the most contemporary challenges to freedom in our own times. This volume is thoughtful, timely, eloquent, engaging, and urgently needed. So, exercise your freedom, and read it."

—R. Albert Mohler Jr., president,
The Southern Baptist Theological Seminary

"If, as Brad Littlejohn thinks, we inhabit 'two parallel worlds of discourse' with regard to freedom, how can the call of freedom be recovered from the wreckage of contemporary rhetoric? Can the heirs of the Protestant Reformation lay hold of the resources to guide them in doing so? This is a book to make you more hopeful about that possibility and yet more aware of the discrimination and thoughtfulness it requires. As you get into each chapter, allow yourself enough time for the complexities that freedom throws in your path. It will be an education you cannot regret."

—Oliver O'Donovan, professor emeritus of Christian ethics and practical theology, University of Edinburgh

"The most pressing battles of our day involve anthropology—our understanding of what it means to be human. From psychology to religion, from sexuality to social order, we are awash in a sea of confusion, and running through all these battles are confused and conflicting notions of freedom. Thankfully, Brad Littlejohn has written a book to untangle the Gordian Knot of Liberty. In this clear and accessible book, Littlejohn shows himself to be a true scribe of the kingdom, bringing out of the storehouse of Christendom treasures old and new, and weaving together spiritual freedom, moral freedom, and political freedom with scholarly and pastoral care. Highly recommended."

—Joseph Rigney, fellow of theology,
New Saint Andrews College

"My friend Brad Littlejohn is a 'mind awake.' In whatever he writes, he always gives you pause for consideration. *Called to Freedom* is a marvelous volume looking at freedom's true meaning set against its counterfeits. Using his gifts and training in both history and moral theology, Littlejohn helps us see that liberty is not autonomy for autonomy's sake. True freedom is the freedom to conform ourselves to God. Littlejohn is a trusted guide in helping Christians understand the connection between spiritual freedom and true political freedom."

—Andrew T. Walker, associate professor of Christian ethics, The Southern Baptist Theological Seminary

CALLED
to
FREEDOM

CALLED *to* FREEDOM

RETRIEVING CHRISTIAN LIBERTY
IN AN AGE OF LICENSE

BRAD LITTLEJOHN

Called to Freedom: Retrieving Christian Liberty in an Age of License
Copyright © 2025 by W. Bradford Littlejohn

Published by B&H Academic®
Brentwood, Tennessee

All rights reserved.

ISBN: 978-1-0877-7950-8

Dewey Decimal Classification: 234
Subject Heading: SALVATION \ GRACE (THEOLOGY) \ FORGIVENESS OF SIN

Unless otherwise noted, all Scripture quotations are taken from The Holy Bible, English Standard Version. ESV® Text Edition: 2016. Copyright © 2001 by Crossway Bibles, a publishing ministry of Good News Publishers.

Scripture quotations marked KJV are taken from the Holy Bible, King James Version (public domain).

Scripture quotations marked NASB are from the New American Standard Bible®, Copyright © 1960, 1971, 1977, 1995, 2020 by The Lockman Foundation. All rights reserved.

The web addresses referenced in this book were live and correct at the time of the book's publication but may be subject to change.

Cover design by Brian Bobel. Cover image: *Wall Street Ferry Ship* by Colin Campbell Cooper, sourced from David Findlay Jr. Fine Art, NYC, USA / Bridgeman Images.

Printed in the United States of America

30 29 28 27 26 25 VP 1 2 3 4 5 6 7 8 9 10

To my daughter, Philippa Hope, whose grey eyes, golden locks, and miraculous fiddle playing are a daily reminder of God's unsparing goodness to me

CONTENTS

Acknowledgments   xiii

Chapter 1: What Is Freedom?   1
Chapter 2: The Great Deliverance:
    Spiritual Freedom in Christ   21
Chapter 3: Walking by the Spirit: The Quest
    for Moral Freedom   43
Chapter 4: Between Right and Rights:
    Making Sense of Political Freedom   63
Chapter 5: Freedom and Technology:
    The Faustian Bargain of Modern Life   85
Chapter 6: Freedom and the Market: Escaping
    the Bondage of Mammon   105
Chapter 7: Freedom and Faith: Getting Real
    about Religious Liberty   125

Conclusion   145
Selected Bibliography   153
Subject Index   163
Scripture Index   173

ACKNOWLEDGMENTS

In many ways, the little book before you has been more than sixteen years in the making. Since almost the beginning of my academic journey at the intersection of Christian theology, ethics, political theory, and Reformation history, I have been wrestling with the meaning of *freedom*, that word that springs so readily to our lips and so rarely pauses to sojourn in our intellects. The first time I recall seriously wrestling with the tensions inherent in modern ideals of liberty was my encounter with William T. Cavanaugh's brilliant little book, *Being Consumed*, in 2007. I am grateful to him for setting me on what will surely prove a lifelong quest to make sense of the paradox of freedom. I am also grateful to my professors at that time—Douglas Wilson, Douglas Jones, and above all Peter Leithart—for prodding, questioning, and arguing as I sought to articulate my early wrestlings.

My most significant intellectual debt, however, is surely to Oliver O'Donovan. Not only did he blaze many of the conceptual trails along which I travel in this book (and in most of my writings, for that matter), but at the University of Edinburgh he supervised my doctoral work, which sought to make sense of the conflicts between Christian liberty and political authority in the red-hot crucible of the English Reformation. That work was eventually published as *The Peril and Promise of Christian Liberty* (Eerdmans, 2017) and remains the foundation for much of what I seek to expound more pithily here. In the decade since that dissertation, I have continued to take regular soundings into the different concepts of liberty in the classical, medieval, early modern, and modern worlds and to frame helpful categories for explaining these concepts, first to myself and then to the contemporary church. At every turn, I have been helped immeasurably by the army of friends at the Davenant Institute, a band of comrades and scholars whom I count it the great privilege of my life to have journeyed alongside. In particular, I want to thank Brad Belschner, Peter Escalante, Steven Wedgeworth, Andrew Fulford, Alastair Roberts, Joseph Minich, Ben Miller, Jake Meador, Scott Pryor, Nathan Hitchen, Susannah Black Roberts, Colin Redemer, Onsi Kamel, Michael Lucchese, Aaron Rothermel, Joe Rigney, Timon Cline, and Nathan Johnson for their friendship, guidance, spiritual encouragement, and vigorous intellectual stimulation on the topics in this book (and many other topics) over the past ten years.

Within the past five years, I have been blessed by a series of employers who also served as great mentors and friends, commissioning me to write on the topics explored here and relentlessly pushing me to refine my arguments and my rhetoric: Mark Mitchell of Patrick Henry College, Yoram Hazony of the Edmund Burke Foundation, and Ryan Anderson of the Ethics and Public Policy Center. Chris DeMuth and Joe Capizzi have also been wonderful mentors and stimulating conversation partners, without whom I don't know where I would be today. Since

I write in order to think, I am deeply indebted to the many editors who have given me a chance to think out loud by publishing my work on these topics over the past few years and who have helped me to improve both my reasoning and my prose in the process: Mark McDowell at *Reformation21*, Jake Meador at *Mere Orthodoxy*, Onsi Kamel at *Ad Fontes*, Julius Krein at *American Affairs*, Yuval Levin at *National Affairs*, Ben Dunson at *American Reformer*, Serena Sigillito at *The Public Discourse*, Andrew Walker at *WORLD Opinions*, and many more. The chapters here represent the best of those many essays and scattered reflections, distilled and refined into a synthesis that I hope will be useful to a wide range of readers.

I am very grateful to Benjamin Quinn and Dennis Greeson of B&H Academic for reaching out to me to propose this project and for helping shepherd it through to completion, graciously offering at least two deadline extensions and (in Ben's case) extensive feedback on the draft manuscript. Above all, I want to thank Onsi Kamel and Nathan Johnson, who both meticulously read through my initial drafts of each chapter and offered invaluable feedback throughout. The book is far better for their suggestions, and the defects that remain should be chalked up to my incorrigibility.

The greatest acknowledgments, however, must be reserved for my family: my grandfather, who taught me to "seek . . . first the kingdom of God" (Matt 6:33 KJV); my father, who first taught me to ask good questions; my mother, who first taught me how to write; and my amazing wife, Rachel, who has for fifteen years taught me the true meaning of love, patience, forgiveness, and hard work. Our marriage is a gift that just keeps on giving, deepening with each year, and there is scarcely a thought in this book that Rachel hasn't listened to me hash out many times, posing helpful questions and offering valuable suggestions at every turn. My four children—Soren, Pippa, Oliver, and Eleanor—though they may have interrupted the writing of this book countless times, have also brightened so many of the moments in between, reminding me of the great truth of the gospel that we find the truest freedom in sacrificial self-giving, planting seeds that will bear fruit thirty-, sixty-, and a hundredfold. May this book be such a seed.

Soli Deo Gloria
Davenant House
Holy Cross Day, 2023

1

What Is Freedom?

> For freedom Christ has set us free; stand firm therefore, and do not submit again to a yoke of slavery.
> —Galatians 5:1

> You keep using that word. I don't think it means what you think it means.
> —Inigo Montoya, *The Princess Bride*

Slaves of Desire or Slaves of Righteousness?

"Who will set me free from this body of death?" (Rom 7:24 NASB) cried the apostle Paul at the climactic point of his great unfolding of the gospel in Romans 5–8. This lament echoes as loudly in our ears today as it did for his Roman readers, even if we have abolished the grotesque institution of slavery whose ugly stain was visible in every Roman villa and marketplace. The desire for freedom pulsates deep in the heart of every human being, as does the nagging sensation that, no matter how free we may be in theory, we still feel deeply, maddeningly *unfree*. Indeed, the more we clamor for new rights, for the freedom to make our own choices, the more we are liable to feel enslaved by those same choices. The more we succeed in getting the "free market" we may have lobbied for, the more we are apt to feel betrayed and disillusioned, oppressed by the very market forces we have unleashed. The more we exercise our freedom of self-government to vote for our representatives, the more we are apt to chafe under the laws they pass and the restrictions they impose.

Paul answered his own question: "The law of the Spirit of life has set you free in Christ Jesus from the law of sin and death" (Rom 8:2). Yet the bondage continues, as the whole creation waits to be "set free from its bondage to corruption and obtain the freedom of the glory of the children of God" (Rom 8:21). Paradoxes abound throughout this passage. We have been set free from sin (Rom 6:7; 8:2), yet we go on sinning. We have been set free, while the whole creation, of which we are a part, continues to groan in bondage. What's more, we are set free by a *law*, which rings oddly in our ears, and we are set free by becoming "slaves of righteousness" (Rom 6:18), which rings more oddly still.

It turns out that bondage of some kind is inescapable. We will all serve somebody or something. It is only a question of whom and how. Some forms of service turn out to be liberating, while some forms of purported freedom turn out to be enslaving and dehumanizing.

The apostle Paul knew a thing or two about freedom and slavery. He was, after all, a Roman citizen, a status to which he appealed several times in the book of Acts. As such, he enjoyed a freedom that was not shared by many inhabitants of the first-century Mediterranean world, a freedom guaranteed and constituted by Roman law and the privileges it conferred. Had he used this freedom as did most of his fellow citizens, he would have purchased slaves. As Richard Bauckham writes, "To be free [in the ancient world] meant to be a master, and therefore, to have slaves. So rulers were free at the expense of their subjects, masters at the expense of their slaves, the rich and powerful at the expense of the poor and vulnerable, men at the expense of women."[1] Paul, however, completely inverted this formula. For him, to be free *was to be a slave*—a slave of Christ (Rom 6:18; 1 Cor 7:22; Eph 6:6). And Paul practiced what he preached. Rather than using his status as a Roman freeman to enslave others, he lived out his Christian vocation as a bondman of Christ Jesus.

In all this, Paul summoned the church to carry out its vocation as the new Israel, which had been set free from bondage in Egypt to become slaves of the Most High. Precisely because of this great corporate liberation, the Israelites were not to hold one another as slaves; precisely because the Israelites were slaves of God, they ought not be slaves of anyone else. For Israel, then, freedom did not mean mastery but service. And the same was true even more of the church, liberated from the even greater bondage of sin—so argued Paul in Romans. Of course, just as Scripture describes Israel not only as God's

---

[1] Richard Bauckham, *God and the Crisis of Freedom: Biblical Commentary and Contemporary Perspectives* (Louisville, KY: Westminster John Knox, 2002), 10.

bondservant but also as his free son, so Paul exhorted the New Israel: "You are no longer a slave, but a son, and if a son, then an heir through God" (Gal 4:7). Paradoxically, the Christian is both slave and son—just as the eternal Son of God made himself the servant of all (Phil 2:7). Or as Martin Luther puts it so memorably in his Reformation masterpiece, *The Freedom of a Christian*, "A Christian is a perfectly free lord of all, subject to none. A Christian is a perfectly dutiful servant of all, subject to all."[2]

Today, we are just as obsessed and preoccupied with freedom as any slave on a Roman estate, dreaming amid slavery's drudgery of a chance to escape or buy his or her freedom. We tell ourselves that we have solved the conundrum of premodern society. For the Romans, some could only be free by enslaving others. For us, freedom and equality have been reconciled: every individual is his or her own master and, increasingly, not the master only over one's own body, but through the power of ever-expanding technology, master over nature, master over time and space. Or is one? Increasingly, the abolition of man's bondage to nature seems to mean, as C. S. Lewis foresaw, the abolition of man. The more we quest for godlike freedom, the more we find slavery reappearing around every corner.

This appears in obvious and mundane ways: my freedom to choose among hundreds of different tennis shoes, purchased for the value of a few hours' labor, depends on the bondage of sweatshop laborers on the other side of the world; and the apparently godlike freedom I enjoy to have the whole world at my fingertips on a smartphone turns out to be at the mercy of a

---

[2] Martin Luther, *The Freedom of a Christian*, in *Three Treatises*, 2nd rev. ed., trans. W. A. Lambert, rev. Harold J. Grimm (Philadelphia: Fortress, 1970), 277.

small cohort of programmers and their all-powerful algorithms. "From this point of view," observes Lewis, "what we call Man's power over Nature turns out to be a power exercised by some men over other men with nature as its instrument."[3] But the problem runs deeper than that—much deeper, as the examples above suggest.

It was the Faustian bargain of modernity to try to make all men free by making all men consumers. As buyers, spenders, and choosers amid an ever-expanding array of products and as browsers through now-infinite digital spaces, we thought we would enjoy the original freedom and equality that were Adam and Eve's the moment they first opened their eyes upon a garden of delights. But we are not in Eden, and even there, possibility was bounded by constraint; freedom was bounded by law. Having said to one another, "Take and eat anything that is a delight to your eyes" (cf. Gen 3:6), we have merely rediscovered our bondage to our own unchained desires. Increasingly rejecting every claim of objective goodness as an impediment to the freedom of self-realization, we have left ourselves with nothing to guide us but desire or, as Lewis says, "obedience to impulse (and therefore, in the long run, to mere 'nature')."[4] Indeed, fearful somehow that we will not be free enough until we consume enough, we put ourselves at the mercy of advertisers and algorithms that will seek to stroke and stoke every desire until it drives us mad. Thus, "man's conquest of Nature turns out, in the moment of its consummation, to be Nature's conquest of Man."[5]

---

[3] C. S. Lewis, *The Abolition of Man* (New York: Macmillan, 1960), 35.
[4] Lewis, 42.
[5] Lewis, 43.

"Do what feels right," our world exhorts us; so we do it, and yet it feels wrong. "For I do not understand my own actions. For I do not do what I want, but I do the very thing I hate" (Rom 7:15). Paul was right. Bondage is inescapable. You can be in bondage to another individual or in bondage to yourself and your desires (and thus, ultimately, to others who have the power to stoke or satisfy those desires) or in bondage to God (and thus, paradoxically, free). As servants of Christ, we have been called to freedom (Gal 5:1). How can we stand firm and not submit again to the yoke of slavery that our democratic, technological age with its mirage of freedom shimmering in the ever-receding distance would impose on us?

In this book, we will consider what it means to cultivate anew the authentic freedom of a Christian in an age that, seeking ever-greater freedom, has stumbled into some of the worst forms of bondage. In short, I will argue that our culture, although constantly giving lip service to "freedom," has lost sight of what the word really means, ignoring millennia of reflection on the spiritual, moral, and political conditions for maintaining true freedom. Of course, this is not entirely our fault; freedom has always been an elusive idea, meaning very different things to different people over the centuries. Let's survey a few ideas about freedom.

The Shifting Ideal of Freedom

For Martin Luther, the "freedom" most worth having was the freedom from works-righteousness (that is, salvation achieved and maintained by one's good deeds), which brought peace before God, and for Martin Luther King Jr., the "freedom" for which he cried in his "I Have a Dream" speech was the freedom from oppression and discrimination, bringing peace between races. In the American Revolution, Patrick Henry declared, "Give me liberty or give me death,"[6] but the liberty he had in mind was clearly not the same liberty that the philosopher John Stuart Mill influentially championed nearly a century later in "On Liberty". Patrick Henry demanded the liberty of political communities to govern themselves by their own laws; Mill demanded the liberty of individuals from laws that squelched their individuality. In the American Civil War, both sides raised a battle cry of freedom: for the South, it was the freedom from Northern interference in their "domestic institutions"; for the North, it was, among other issues, the freedom of African American slaves who were being ground into the dust by those institutions. During the Great Depression, Franklin Delano Roosevelt repurposed the venerable ideal, summoning Americans to guarantee their fellow citizens' "freedom from want"—that is, economic security, steady employment, and a living wage. Just a few years later, however, political philosopher Friedrich Hayek denounced government efforts to manage economic outcomes as the single greatest *threat* to freedom, which he understood as every individual's right to make his or her own economic choices. This same clash between different visions of economic freedom resurfaced in the aftermath of the 2008 Great Recession, as President Barack Obama attempted to rekindle Roosevelt's commitment to provide "freedom from want" for struggling Americans, provoking the Tea

---

[6] Patrick Henry, "Give Me Liberty or Give Me Death," March 23, 1775, https://www.ushistory.org/documents/libertydeath.htm.

Party movement as a backlash in defense of a Hayekian view of free markets. Even more recently, the Covid-19 pandemic pitted different visions of freedom against one another: for some it was the freedom to enter public places without undue fear of infection (which required policies like mandated masking, vaccines, or social distancing), while for others it was the freedom to make their own medical decisions without interference.

Confronted with such a dizzying array of claims on behalf of "liberty" or "freedom" (note that I will use the two words interchangeably in this book), we might well wonder whether the words have any usable meaning at all. Is "freedom" perhaps a mere slogan that can be adapted for any political or religious agenda, a wax nose that can be bent to the orator's whims? I do not think so. Certainly, the term can be stretched beyond recognition in pursuit of particular agendas, but ordinarily, we can recognize a resemblance between different versions of the ideal. All of these versions center on our distinctive human ability to exercise moral agency, which is our capacity for purposeful or meaningful action. (*Meaningful* action, of course, requires communication within a community; I cannot really enjoy "freedom of speech" in a context where no one speaks my language.) This capacity—which makes us different from animals and is part of what it means to be God's image bearers—can be threatened in innumerable different ways, and each of these threats, when it appears, is thus experienced as an attack on freedom. This explains why we are apt to invoke "freedom" in such varied (and occasionally contradictory) contexts. As Oliver O'Donovan observes, "Freedom is the looking glass in which we search our features anxiously for signs of 'unfreedom.' But the collapse of any vital condition can occur in a multitude of ways, so what appear to be straightforward descriptions of freedom turn out to be hugely various political ideals, some of them in tension with others."[7]

From this vantage point it is no surprise that our conceptions of freedom can be as varied and numerous as the different directions from which freedom can be threatened. Isaiah Berlin claims to have chronicled over 200 different definitions of the term.[8] Thankfully, we need not go into all 200 here. It will suffice instead to map the ideal of freedom along three main axes: (1) the tension between *negative* and *positive* liberty, (2) the tension between *individual* and *corporate* liberty, and (3) the tension between *inward* and *outward* liberty. Through a quick survey of this terrain, we will be better able to discern the fault lines bedeviling our search for freedom today. This quick survey will also give us the appropriate starting point for charting a course toward an authentic and enduring experience of Christian freedom.

Mapping Freedom in Three Dimensions

Negative and Positive Liberty

The first of these axes comes from Berlin himself, who in a 1958 lecture, "Two Concepts of Liberty," proposed a basic distinction between "negative liberty" and "positive liberty." The first

---

[7] Oliver O'Donovan, *The Ways of Judgment* (Grand Rapids, MI: Eerdmans, 2005), 68.

[8] Isaiah Berlin, "Two Concepts of Liberty," in *Liberty: Incorporating Four Essays on Liberty*, ed. Henry Hardy (Oxford: Oxford University Press, 2002), 169.

designates "the area within which the subject . . . is or should be left to do or be what he is able to do or be, without interference by other persons."[9] It is then the liberty of "noninterference," the freedom to be left alone, the freedom that each individual in late modern society demands from other individuals and especially from institutions and authorities like the government. This is no doubt the concept of freedom that leaps most quickly to mind and most readily incites political action in our own day, whether invoked on the Left (as in the freedom of "my body, my choice" asserted by abortion-rights advocates) or on the Right (as in the demand for low taxes, deregulation, and private property rights that have been identified with conservatism since the days of Ronald Reagan). Of course, it is far from clear what ought to count as "interference" or "coercion." Many people will contend that any attempt to influence their behavior, including mere moral disapproval, is an attack on their freedom as they conceive it. But without some outside influence to tell us what we should value and what we should shun, we would be entirely directionless, paralyzed with indecision or else lurching randomly in response to passing whims. Hence the need for any such negative liberty to be matched with positive liberty.

When it comes to this latter notion, Berlin's various halting definitions are less clear, but it is not hard to get the gist of his argument. Where negative liberty is "freedom *from*," positive liberty is "freedom *for*" or "freedom *to*." Positive liberty suggests that I am not merely left alone, but I am going somewhere; my actions have a purpose, a direction, a meaning. It is this that great athletes seem to have in mind when they speak of

---

[9] Berlin, 169.

the exhilarating "freedom" they experience when performing at the highest level. It is not that runners or mountain climbers lack constraints—indeed, there may be few situations *more* constraining than those encountered when scaling a cliff with scarcely any handholds—rather, they know that they are fully able to be and to do what they aspire to *within* those constraints. From this perspective, we can see the shortsightedness of our modern imagination that "freedom is constituted by the absence of limits."[10] On the contrary, limits are what makes free action possible. As finite creatures, we cannot cope with infinite possibilities, and even when we do have many possibilities to choose from, we exercise our freedom by limiting ourselves to one. There are many goods that you are only free to enjoy to the extent that you *commit* to them, renouncing all others: a spouse, for instance. Confusion about freedom has consequences, as we see today in our own unhappy age where men and women, fearful that commitment will compromise their freedom, are never free to experience the joy that comes from giving themselves entirely to another.

Individual and Corporate Liberty

If we are afraid that commitment to even one other person might compromise our freedom, how much more so commitment to a community! Yet if we are meant for life in community, as both the book of Genesis (Gen 2:18) and the whole of human experience tell us, then our freedom must be realized in such a common life. Indeed, even nowadays we find that we often think and speak

---

[10] Oliver O'Donovan, *Resurrection and Moral Order: An Outline for Evangelical Ethics*, 2nd ed. (Grand Rapids, MI: Eerdmans, 1994), 107.

in terms of such *corporate liberty*: the liberty of a community to order its common life. When Christians complained of attacks on religious liberty during the COVID-19 pandemic, it was pre-eminently the liberty of entire church communities to gather for worship that concerned them. When the American patriots of the Revolutionary era fought for freedom from Britain, they were fighting not so much for individual liberty but so that each colony could govern itself, passing its own laws and charting its own course as a community. Such quests for national liberty continue to inspire powerful political movements, such as Britain's campaign for "Brexit" from the EU, and acts of extraordinary courage, such as Ukraine's resistance to Russian invasion.

From one perspective, such corporate liberty seems to come only at the expense of individual liberty. For instance, when I gather to worship with my fellow congregants, I must sacrifice any number of personal freedoms in the process. I must submit to the church leadership's decision of when to worship (maybe I'd rather sleep in a bit more), where to worship (maybe I prefer more elegant architecture), and how to worship (maybe I prefer more traditional hymns). In our age of consumeristic church-hopping, I might freely choose a church that suits my tastes. But still, when it comes to the time for hymn-singing, unless every congregant sacrifices his freedom to sing whatever song comes into his head, the congregation as a whole will not be free to worship. This is but one example of a basic but too often neglected truth: an institution or community is only free to act to the extent that it limits the freedom of its members to act on their own preferences.[11] Obviously, this is true at the political

---

[11] For a fuller discussion, see my book *The Peril and Promise of Christian Liberty: Richard Hooker, the Puritans, and Protestant Political*

level as well: Britain could only choose Brexit by overriding the minority who wanted to stay in the EU, and Ukraine could only maintain its independence by ignoring (and perhaps even locking up) the small number of Russian sympathizers in its midst. The American Revolutionaries fought for the freedom to make their own laws—laws that limited the choices of individuals. This point has acquired a new salience in the wake of the *Dobbs* ruling in America overturning a federally guaranteed right to abortion. On one side of the political divide now are those fighting for the freedom of each woman to choose whether to continue her pregnancy; on the other side are those who contend that states, as moral communities, ought to be free to restrict the murder of unborn children.

This tension between corporate and individual liberty may be eased to some extent by the role of imagination. After all, only the most pathological amongst us actually conceive of ourselves as mere solitary individuals. Rather, because we were created for one another, we are apt to experience others as comprising what we might call an "extended self": first our close family members, then perhaps our friends and church community, and finally in some measure our entire nation. This was perhaps truer in premodern society, which was apt to think in terms of families, tribes, and clans; but even today, we are far less individualist than we imagine.[12] Even those seemingly most committed to the modern ideal of radical individual freedom,

---

Theology (Grand Rapids, MI: Eerdmans, 2017), especially chaps. 2 and 4.

[12] For these insights, I am particularly indebted to the profound discussion in chap. 3 of Yoram Hazony, *Conservatism: A Rediscovery* (New York: Regnery, 2022).

such as LGBT activists, are liable to experience an attack on any member of the "LGBT+ community" as an attack on themselves. Thus, in a healthy and well-integrated community, we will not tend to think of the institution being free to act *at the expense of* its members, but rather of its members being free to act *in*, *through*, and *as* the institution.

Still, with all these qualifiers, we cannot shake the sense that there is an intrinsically competitive dimension to freedom as we have discussed it thus far. We observed this right at the outset: in the Roman world, everyone aspired to the freedom of a citizen, but this was ordinarily a freedom exercised at the expense of the bondage of slaves. Today, we may have formally given freedom to everyone in our societies, but the reality is that I am only able to exercise my freedom to the extent that I do not trespass on yours or inflict harm on you. Sometimes this is comparatively straightforward (I am not free to beat you to a bloody pulp for kicks), while sometimes it is anything but (am I free to refuse baking a cake for a same-sex couple, or is this a form of psychological assault on them?). Some of these interpersonal conflicts may be subsumed within the higher freedom that a whole community or nation enjoys, but even at this level, competition is not banished: each nation's freedom to act will limit every nation's freedom to act.

Inward and Outward Liberty

There is only one domain where this concern does not apply: the internal domain. We must thus conclude with a third distinction: that between *inward* and *outward freedom*. Such a distinction is a precarious one, to be sure. Body and soul make up one inseparable whole, and we should not deceive ourselves into thinking that we can neatly distinguish, much less separate, the internal and external domains. However, if this distinction is a difficult one, it is nonetheless essential if we are not to run headlong into incoherence. In the 1992 Supreme Court decision on abortion rights, *Planned Parenthood v. Casey*, Justices Anthony Kennedy, Sandra Day O'Connor, and David Souter famously declared, "At the heart of liberty is the right to define one's own concept of existence, of meaning, of the universe, and of the mystery of human life."[13] In the 2022 case overturning *Roe* and *Casey*, Justice Samuel Alito acidly retorted, "While individuals are certainly free to think and to say what they wish about 'existence,' 'meaning,' the 'universe,' and 'the mystery of human life,' they are not always free to act in accordance with those thoughts."[14] After all, many people throughout history have thought that the mystery of human life found its fulfillment in the sacrifice of some human lives to placate the gods, but presumably we ought not permit them to indulge that freedom today. More relevantly, perhaps, many people find "meaning" in dark and violent sexual fantasies, but it would be absurd to say that since we cannot stop them *thinking* such things, they must have the freedom to act them out.

There is a natural freedom within the human mind that no human power can take away: a freedom to form thought and beliefs, entertain desires, and form purposes. This freedom

---

[13] *Planned Parenthood of Southeastern Pa. v. Casey*, 505 U.S. 833 (1992), 851, https://supreme.justia.com/cases/federal/us/505/833/.

[14] *Dobbs v. Jackson Women's Health Organization*, 597 U.S. ___ (2022), 1, https://supreme.justia.com/cases/federal/us/597/19-1392/.

can operate amid even the most profound external oppression. Indeed, it is in such circumstances that the power of the human spirit shines through most vividly: no matter what others may do to us, each of us retains the power to place our own meaning on our own circumstances. Consider Paul and Silas in the Philippian prison: while the jailer thought that he had them in his power, they were cheerfully "praying and singing hymns to God," so free in the midst of their bondage that when an earthquake burst the prison doors open, they saw no reason to run away (Acts 16:25–28). A secular form of such inner freedom is captured in the poem "Invictus," made famous by Nelson Mandela's recitation of it in Robben Island Prison: "In the fell clutch of circumstance / I have not winced nor cried aloud. / Under the bludgeonings of chance / My head is bloody, but unbowed. . . . It matters not how strait the gate, / How charged with punishments the scroll, / I am the master of my fate: / I am the captain of my soul."[15] Paul would disagree, of course; fallen man lies captive to sin, and redeemed man submits to the Lord Christ as captain of his soul. Still, these words can be true in a relative sense, and even for unbelievers, such inner freedom can be a source of strength amid profound adversity.

Such inward liberty, crucially, is not trapped within the zero-sum logic that bedevils every other form of freedom. To be sure, many people's freedom may coexist peacefully most of the time, or even harmonize within the higher freedom experienced by a tight-knit community, but at some point, it will always bump up against the limit of others' freedom in ways both trivial and

---

[15] William Earnest Henley, "Invictus," Poets.org, accessed April 23, 2024, https://poets.org/poem/invictus.

profound. My freedom to hum a tune may disturb your freedom to enjoy a quiet walk, and your freedom to flaunt your transgressive sexual identity will clash with my freedom to raise a family within a stable moral culture. My inner freedom to form and cling to my own convictions and to calmly face the trials of life in light of these convictions will never conflict—at least *directly*—with your freedom to do the same. This observation only gets us so far, of course. After all, there are myriad ways in which we can indirectly compromise someone's inward liberty: by propaganda, manipulation, seduction, or intimidation. And an inward liberty that can *never* express itself outwardly (for instance, a freedom to believe in Jesus but never to gather with other believers for public worship) is a contradiction in terms.

Nonetheless, even if inward liberty cannot last long without at least some outward liberty, authentic outward liberty cannot exist *at all* in the absence of inner freedom. If freedom is the capacity for meaningful action, it must always begin with an *I*, an agent, capable of forming purposes and acting upon them. A person whose mind is in bondage, like those poor souls subjected to the unforgivable "Imperius curse" in J. K. Rowling's *Harry Potter* books, or indeed the twisted souls of those who would do this to another human, can never be considered free, whatever wealth and opportunities they might possess. Any discussion of freedom, then, must begin here, at the center, in the human heart. The apostle Paul had it right: unless we can be free from the bondage of sin within, we will never be free in any sense that really matters, nor will we be able to bring freedom to others. Our own day has gotten it backward: trading liberty for license, we have accepted a profound unfreedom of soul and spirit in return for the false promise of limitless external freedom.

Frustrated by our sense of futility and by the inevitable limits that come from sharing a world with other human beings, we are tempted to lash out at one another, against the authorities God has placed above us, or at God himself for interfering with our liberty. Professing to be free, we have become slaves, and we have exchanged the glory of incorruptible life before God with an ignoble bondage to mortal man and creeping things. Yet the less liberty we feel, the more liberty we demand, without knowing anymore what it is we are asking for.

A Road Map for This Book

In this book, I will offer a brief guide for Christians struggling to understand and live out the freedom of a Christian in an age of license. Against the false freedom promised by our age's exhortations to "follow your heart," I present an alternative account of freedom that navigates among the various poles I've sketched out above.

Beginning with the inward dimension of freedom, I will discuss the *spiritual freedom* promised by Christ, preached by the apostles, proclaimed anew in the liberating message of the Protestant Reformation, and fully enjoyed by the justified believer. This freedom is both negative (from the curse of the law) and positive (toward the love of God and neighbor) and is experienced only by the Christian individual, however much the corporate community of the church may contribute.

Next, I will consider the *moral freedom* that flows from this spiritual freedom as the fruit of the Spirit's work enabling us by his constant aid and concurrence to subdue the flesh, master our desires, and do the good that we want to do (see Rom 7:19).

This liberty begins within but expresses itself outwardly, through the lives of both individuals and communities. It has both negative and positive dimensions, as we break free from the entanglements of sin and the manipulations of others to be who we were truly meant to be. Even unbelievers can experience some echo of this freedom by self-discipline and self-mastery, but ultimately it too belongs only to the Christian keeping "in step with the Spirit" (Gal 5:25).

Finally, there is the *political freedom* that has often preoccupied us moderns, an external freedom from bondage to other men, the freedom to chart our own course as individuals, communities, or nations. Although we often talk only about the individual and negative dimensions of this freedom, it has corporate and positive dimensions too. Today we often seek this freedom as an end in itself, forgetting that it is only a means to higher ends. Today, also, we often imagine that it can be pursued and achieved on its own, while in fact it is wholly dependent on an underlying foundation of spiritual and moral freedom. A people in bondage to sin, death, and fear will only ever have a pale shadow of political freedom.

Having outlined these three distinct domains of freedom, I will conclude the book with three case studies of what Christian freedom means today, how we get it wrong, and how it is under threat. Chapter 5 will consider the role of technology, which promises greater freedom but often delivers us up to slavery. Chapter 6 will discuss the problem of "free markets" and rival visions of what it means to pursue authentic economic freedom in a world of sin and scarcity. Chapter 7, finally, will tackle the problem of religious liberty, which has become an urgent preoccupation again for many Christians in the modern West, who have awoken to the realization that their fellow citizens no longer understand or value this freedom as they once did.

At the conclusion of his glorious presentation of the gospel of liberty in Romans, Paul tells us how we should then live in light of this good news. The first step is to clear our heads: "Do not be conformed to this world, but *be transformed by the renewal of your mind*, that by testing you may discern what is the will of God, what is good and acceptable and perfect" (Rom 12:2; emphasis added). The Romans, like us today, had their minds filled with confused and confusing ideas of freedom and slavery, worldly notions that impaired their ability to cast off sin and run the race of righteousness. If we today are to experience anew "the freedom of the glory of the children of God" (Rom 8:21), we must begin by renewing our minds—by testing the different ideals of freedom that the world presents to us and discerning God's will so that we might learn to "walk by the Spirit and . . . not gratify the desires of the flesh" (Gal 5:16). For "the Lord is the Spirit, and where the Spirit of the Lord is, there is freedom" (2 Cor 3:17).

2

The Great Deliverance: Spiritual Freedom in Christ

> There is therefore now no condemnation
> for those who are in Christ Jesus.
> —Romans 8:1

Q: What is your only comfort in life and in death?

A: That I am not my own, but belong, body and soul, in life and in death, not to myself, but to my faithful Savior Jesus Christ, who at the cost of his own blood has fully paid for all my sins and completely freed me from the dominion of the devil.
—Heidelberg Catechism, Q. 1

Forgetfulness, Futility, and Fear

Although freedom has many dimensions, all true freedom must start by resolving the problem at the heart of human existence:

the alienation between God and man due to sin. If freedom is, as I have defined it, "the capacity for meaningful action," then no wonder the Scriptures describe sin as slavery; for sin strips us of this capacity, separating us not only from God, the source of all ultimate meaning, but also from ourselves and our own purposes. But we must be clear that there are two distinct problems here. There are individual actions of sin, which represent a bondage of the will to false notions and disordered desires. This bondage creates a moral slavery that good teaching and good habits can partially overcome but from which only the sanctifying work of the Spirit can truly free us. We will consider this problem in chapter 3. The more fundamental problem, which is addressed by God's gracious act of justification, is that we live in a *condition* of sin, under the power of sin, resulting in a spiritual bondage from which Christ alone can set us free. In this chapter, we will consider the nature of this bondage and how the gospel liberates us from it. We'll then take some time to discuss the dangers that can arise when this spiritual freedom is confused with the moral and political freedoms that flow from it.

The power of sin causes us to lose our freedom, our capacity for meaningful action, in three main ways: forgetfulness, futility, and fear. With the first, *forgetfulness*, sin cuts us off from our *past*, which provides us a sense of agency. Indeed, there are few experiences more disorienting and terrifying than being told we have done something of which we have no recollection. Yet if the past is a source of guilt, as it is for every sinner, we may seek to escape from it, hiding ourselves and dulling our memories in fresh acts of sin. Drugs and alcohol are simply the most vivid forms of such self-obliteration. The momentary "freedom" of such escape is indeed a Faustian bargain;[1] the individual may evade the burden of painful responsibility but at the cost of losing a unified selfhood.

Second, there is what, for lack of a better word, I have called *futility*, by which the *present* is rendered unintelligible to us. This can take several forms. Often, we can still form purposes, but we feel totally unable to realize them. Whatever good we seek to do, we do not do; it is as if some alien power has co-opted our mind and body. Other times, we succeed in achieving what we thought we wanted, surrounding ourselves with pleasures and achievements, only to find that they, too, are empty vapor—the constant theme of the book of Ecclesiastes. Either way, this futility, whether the result of sin, external circumstances, or indeed chemical imbalances, can develop into the phenomenon of depression, which in extreme forms can result in an almost total paralysis of agency; an individual in such a state becomes convinced that there is no point in trying to act. Or perhaps "convinced" isn't even the right word, implying as it does a free pathway of reasoning. Those locked in the throes of depression can experience a numbness that suffocates thought itself.

Martin Luther was no stranger to any of these. Indeed, many modern scholars surmise that the *anfechtungen*, the dark nights of the soul he often experienced, were at least partially the result of what we now diagnose as clinical depression. This does not, however, detract from the spiritual reality of these

---

[1] The protagonist of a German legend famously rendered by Marlowe (1592) and Goethe (1808), Faust made a pact with the devil, selling his soul in exchange for power, knowledge, and pleasure.

experiences. Let us say rather that clinical depression is simply a vivid manifestation of our sin nature, an intensified expression of the spiritual deadness in which we all languish without Christ and which even Christians continue to wrestle with in this life. In Luther's early masterpiece, *The Freedom of a Christian* (1520), he outlines the true contours of spiritual freedom as a response to the threats of forgetfulness, futility, and fear.

By the last, *fear*, we are blockaded from the *future* because of our terror of what lies ahead. Indeed, it is worth stressing that the great majority of what we ordinarily call "coercion" is strictly speaking just intimidation, the threat of future harm. I say "just" intimidation, even though it is in many ways more crippling than true coercion. If I am in chains, I may be physically compelled to go from point A to point B, but my mind may be free all the while—to scheme of escape, to sing hymns of praise to God like Paul and Silas, or simply to take in the beauty of my surroundings. If, however, I am cowed by fear of death or torture, I may find myself unable to think straight, unable to form any purposes beyond the current moment.

The Great Deliverance of the Gospel

Let us begin with the last of these, fear. Scripture describes the "fear of death" as the root of the sinner's "lifelong slavery" (Heb 2:15). Indeed, many people, whether in pandemics or war zones, have found themselves paralyzed by this fear, unable to act. The threat of physical death is perhaps the preeminent way that tyrants take away the freedom of their subjects. People can, however, be trained to master this fear by learning to value something else more than mere physical life. Scripture shows us that the true fear of death holding us in bondage is the fear of eternal death (Matt 10:28). It is this death that is the wages of sin (Rom 6:23), and it is this death that we are constantly seeking to escape through our good works.

As Luther powerfully argues, however, following Paul in Galatians 5, any attempt to escape this fear by our own deeds will be self-defeating. We will never be able to do enough to keep the doubts at bay; even in our best works, we will be hounded by the fear that those works are not good enough, and to the extent that we do good works *in order to be saved*, we may have a nagging sense that this self-absorption taints their goodness. This is why Luther goes so far as to say, "This faith cannot exist in connection with works—that is to say, if you at the same time claim to be justified by works, whatever their character—for that would be the same as 'limping with two different opinions' [1 Kings 18:21]."[2] It is not that the believer is saved from doing good works, but he *is* saved from the *burden* of doing good works as a means to eternal life. So long as we perceive our works this way, we remain under the curse of the law, as a form of bondage, not a word of liberation: "For all who rely on works of the law are under a curse" (Gal 3:10), and "you are severed from Christ, you who would be justified by the law; you have fallen away from grace" (Gal 5:4). The Christian, however, writes Luther, "is free from all things and over all things so that he needs no works to make him righteous and save him, since faith alone abundantly

---

[2] Martin Luther, *The Freedom of a Christian*, in *Three Treatises*, 2nd rev. ed., trans. W. A. Lambert, rev. Harold J. Grimm (Philadelphia: Fortress, 1970), 280.

confers all these things."[3] By receiving the word of promise, by which Christ promises to cover all our sins and deliver us once for all from both physical and spiritual death, we experience the deepest inward freedom, able to hold our heads high knowing that "there is therefore now no condemnation for those who are in Christ Jesus" (Rom 8:1).

By this means, we are released also from the bondage of futility, in which we never feel sure whether our actions really matter or mean anything. This, too, is the effect of sin, and nothing but faith can cure it. Luther asserts, "It is evident that no external thing has any influence in producing Christian righteousness of freedom, or in producing unrighteousness of servitude."[4] In other words, the experience of profound depression—in which we feel as if nothing we do makes any difference—is actually a disclosure of spiritual reality. Left to our own devices, nothing we do *can* make any difference in an ultimate and eternal sense.

> What can it profit the soul if the body is well, free, and active, and eats, drinks, and does as it pleases? For in these respects even the most godless slaves of vice may prosper. . . . It does not help the soul if the body is adorned with the sacred robes of priests or dwells in sacred places or is occupied with sacred duties or prays, fasts, abstains from certain kinds of food, or does any work that can be done by the body and in the body. The righteousness and the freedom of the soul require something far different.[5]

---

[3] Luther, 291.
[4] Luther, 278.
[5] Luther, 279.

Every conceivable kind of externally good work is only *potentially* good; in itself, it could be thoroughly rotten and corrupt.

Of course, the flip side of this, which may be a great comfort, is that if nothing we do ourselves can help the soul, likewise nothing that is done *to us* can harm the soul: "On the other hand, how will poor health or imprisonment or hunger or thirst or any other external misfortune harm the soul?" asks Luther,[6] echoing Paul's bracing words from Rom 8:35, 37: "Who shall separate us from the love of Christ? Shall tribulation, or distress, or persecution, or famine, or nakedness, or danger, or sword? . . . No, in all these things we are more than conquerors through him who loved us." What a comfort to us in the throes of depression, weighed down by our own failures and limitations, with the arrows and slings of fortune, with the betrayals of friend or the cheated hopes that come from leaning on frail mortal supports! Just as no good work makes any difference in the end unless done in faith, unless first clothed in the righteousness of Christ, so even the weakest, stumbling effort at obedience, when done in faith, is received by God as cleansed of every stain for Christ's sake.

Too often Luther's doctrine of justification is treated in abstraction from his inseparable theology of sanctification. By his doctrine of Christ's "alien righteousness," Luther did not mean that we simply continue in bondage to sin and that God just pretends otherwise—as if Romans 8 represented merely a new way of contextualizing the futility of Romans 7. No, we are enabled by the Spirit to fight and triumph over sin, but precisely because this triumph is always incomplete, we will derive no

---

[6] Luther, 278.

comfort from this work of sanctification without the confidence that Christ sanctifies every tainted work of ours and offers it up to the Father purged of its dross. The freedom of a Christian then is the liberation from the sense of futility that comes from an awareness of our fallenness and finitude.

But how does the freedom of a Christian rescue us from forgetfulness? At first glance, it might seem to do the opposite. Critics of Luther's teaching on justification see it as a bit of divine playacting, in which God, by mere fiat, makes it as if we had never sinned after all, replacing our story with Christ's. Thus Luther wrote:

> As a matter of fact, he makes them his own and acts as if they were his own and as if he himself had sinned; he suffered, died, and descended into hell that he might overcome them all. Now since it was such a one who did all this, and death and hell could not swallow him up, these were necessarily swallowed up by him in a mighty duel; for his righteousness is greater than the sins of all men, his life stronger than death, his salvation more invincible than hell.[7]

Is redemption, then, a blissful forgetfulness of our past sin? No. Sin is, rather, always seeking to cut us off from the truth about ourselves, enticing us to forget God's past grace to us and to forget our own responsibility for our present miserable condition. Sin invites each of us to imagine ourselves merely as victims—a dynamic prominently on display in today's society. So it is that throughout the Old Testament, God constantly seeks to remind

---

[7] Luther, 286–87.

his people—through their judges, prophets, and psalmists—of his past works of deliverance. This is not simply to shame them into repentance—"After all I've done for you!"—but to remind them of their history of sinfulness because repentance is impossible without a true reckoning with the past. This is why, for Luther, the gospel is always preceded by law, a word of condemnation in which we are forced to look in the mirror and tell the truth about ourselves. Only when we know, and own, the depth of our own bondage can we turn to the gospel and be free of that bondage.

Indeed, this basic insight has been taken up by mainstream therapy in Alcoholics Anonymous's "12 Step Program" and related approaches, which represent a secularization of Luther's account of repentance:

1. We admitted we were powerless over alcohol—that our lives had become unmanageable.
2. Came to believe that a Power greater than ourselves could restore us to sanity.
3. Made a decision to turn our will and our lives over to the care of God as we understood Him.[8]

Although these steps, and the rest that follow, will offer no permanent deliverance if detached from the true gospel, they grasp the essential structure of the inward liberation that must precede any genuine moral freedom.

In Luther's understanding, the believer is set free by accepting the alien righteousness of Christ, which cancels the believer's past sin but *only insofar as the believer remembers that this*

---

[8] "The Twelve Steps," *Alcoholics Anonymous*, https://www.aa.org/the-twelve-steps, accessed May 22, 2023.

is the case—that is, that he or she really was truly under condemnation without Christ. Too much Protestant theology nowadays has taken the good news of justification as a casual starting point, rather than as a hard-won conclusion. Christians are exhorted to celebrate their freedom in Christ, to shrug off any feelings of guilt, and to look on God as full of grace only, never wrath. Any reminder that sin deserves damnation is treated as an intrusion of Pharisaism. But this simply cheapens grace and takes it for granted. No, the good news is only good news against the backdrop of bad news about our condition without Christ, and if we allow ourselves to forget that, we will never experience the true freedom of a soul ransomed from the jaws of the dragon by the Savior who is at the same time the soul's bridegroom. As Luther says, "Thus the believing soul by means of the pledge of his faith is free in Christ, its bridegroom, free from all sins, secure against death and hell, and is endowed with the eternal righteousness, life, and salvation of Christ, its bridegroom."[9]

Distinguishing Spiritual Freedom from Moral Freedom

Luther's teaching on Christian liberty was intimately linked to the doctrine of justification by faith, as indeed it was for the apostle Paul in Galatians. By it the Reformers sought to drive out every form of legalism or Pelagianism,[10] in which con-

---

[9] Luther, *Freedom of a Christian*, 287.

[10] Pelagianism is a heresy that derives its name from the British monk Pelagius (354–418), who opposed Augustine over his doctrine of grace. Pelagius was convinced that the sinful human will remained completely free to cooperate with God's grace through good works. His

sciences were burdened by a long list of commands or counsels that must be obeyed in order to attain grace and holiness. Wrongly understood, however, it could open the door for antinomianism or moral relativism,[11] in which believers imagined that sin didn't matter anymore now that they'd been justified. Accordingly, it is important for us to understand that spiritual freedom is not the same as moral freedom—there is still the problem of indwelling sin to be solved after we have heard the word of forgiveness.

Paul himself, of course, faced the challenge of antinomianism in his own teaching: "What shall we say then? Are we to continue in sin that grace may abound?" (Rom 6:1). And it was not long before Luther and the other Reformers were busily combating this misunderstanding. Being freed from bondage to works, Luther cautioned, does not mean being freed from *doing* good works. Quite the contrary.

Luther states the paradox right at the outset of *The Freedom of a Christian*: "A Christian is a perfectly free lord of all, subject to none. A Christian is a perfectly dutiful servant of all, subject

---

teaching was condemned at the Council of Ephesus (431) as amounting to a theology of self-salvation. During the Protestant Reformation and afterward, concerns over Pelagianism (or semi-Pelagianism) reemerged as the Reformers charged that medieval Roman theology had lapsed into similar errors.

[11] Antinomianism (from the Greek meaning "against the law") represents a perennial temptation in Christian theology that comes from stressing only the unconditionality of God's free grace, but it emerged as a particular threat in the early years of the Reformation as a misinterpretation of Luther's teaching. The antinomians taught that, having been set free by faith, the believer did not need to worry about the moral law of God so long as his heart was in the right place.

to all."[12] Precisely because no longer blinded by forgetfulness, futility, and fear, no longer preoccupied with the project of self-salvation, the believer can focus for the first time properly on the needs of his neighbor: "A man does not live for himself alone in this mortal body to work for it alone, but he lives also for all men on earth; rather he lives only for others and not for himself. To this end he brings his body into subjection that he may the more sincerely and freely serve others."[13]

Thus, how we behave in the world still matters immensely—not as something flowing *toward* salvation but as something flowing *from* salvation (cf. Jas 2:14–26). We can still apply moral criteria of good and evil, better or worse, to the actions of redeemed Christians by asking, "Are you living out what God created you to be? Are you using your freedom to serve one another?" Again, Paul's own writing consistently follows this logic. In Galatians 5 he declares, "For you were called to freedom, brothers. Only do not use your freedom as an opportunity for the flesh, but through love serve one another. For the whole law is fulfilled in one word: 'You shall love your neighbor as yourself'" (vv. 13–14). And in several of his epistles, we see a consistent movement from a declaration in the first few chapters of what God has done for us in Christ to an exhortation on how we should live, consistently with this new reality, in the final chapters.

Still, if we simply pivoted directly from the liberating good news of justification to the long hard slog of sanctification, without saying anything more on the subject, our response to the threat of antinomianism would be simply a new legalism. It

---

[12] Luther, *Freedom of a Christian*, 277.
[13] Luther, 301.

is critical, then, that we understand the spiritual freedom of the Christian as transforming the very nature of moral experience.

John Calvin explains this well, in his own treatment of Christian liberty in *The Institutes of the Christian Religion*. There he begins by explaining that Christian liberty has three distinct elements. The first is simply what Luther has described in the first half of *The Freedom of a Christian*: "the consciences of believers, in seeking assurance of their justification before God, should rise above and advance beyond the law, forgetting all law righteousness."[14] The second is that

> consciences observe the law, not as if constrained by the necessity of the law, but that freed from the law's yoke they willingly obey God's will. For since they dwell in perpetual dread so long as they remain under the sway of the law, they will never be eager and ready to obey God unless they have already been given this sort of freedom.[15]

The third we will discuss in the next section.

In other words, the law continues to function in the life of a justified Christian, for even if "love is the fulfilling of the law" (Rom 13:10), love still needs concrete moral guidance, and the law of God provides this. But the law is experienced in a profoundly different way: no longer as a terrifying judge but rather as a benevolent teacher, showing us how to obey God as

---

[14] John Calvin, *The Institutes of the Christian Religion*, ed. John T. McNeill, trans. Ford Lewis Battles, 2 vols. (Louisville: Westminster John Knox, 1960), 1:834 [III.19.2].

[15] Calvin, 1:836 [III.19.4].

we are eager to do. The spiritual freedom of a Christian thus issues in a renewed moral freedom: the blessed effortlessness of knowing the right and doing the right *because you want to*, not because you have to. To be sure, in the lived experience of the regenerate-but-still-sinful believer, this remains more ideal than reality; the flesh still lusts against the Spirit and chafes against the law. We will return in the next chapter to reflect more fully on the progressive experience of moral freedom through the Spirit's sanctifying work.

Distinguishing Spiritual Freedom from Political Freedom

If antinomianism resulted from confusing spiritual and moral freedom, *anarchism* could result from confusing spiritual and political freedom. When Luther railed against the oppression of human authorities (like the pope and his canon lawyers, who bound people's consciences by claiming for themselves divine authority), some heard him issuing a rebuke to any exercise of human authority. Indeed, Luther soon had his hands full managing some of the political chaos that grew out the distortion of his work, a distortion that continued to bedevil Protestants throughout the century and down to the present day. According to the teaching of many evangelicals today, Christian liberty consists in the freedom of each individual believer to make up his own mind and to frame his own behavior however he wants in any matters where God has not spoken in Scripture. Any human authority, whether in church or state, is accused of violating Christian liberty if they dare to issue particular commands (or even sometimes attempt to offer strong guidance) in such matters. We saw this frequently, for instance, during the coronavirus pandemic.

Few, however, seem to realize just how destructive the logic of this position is. As Richard Hooker would write toward the end of the sixteenth century:

> [This] opinion, albeit applied here no further than to this present cause, shaketh universally the fabric of government, tendeth to anarchy and mere confusion, dissolveth families, dissipateth colleges, corporations, armies, overthroweth kingdoms, churches, and whatsoever is now through the providence of God by authority and power upheld.[16]

This seems a bit melodramatic at first, but Hooker goes on to explain that it is, after all, the primary function of parents, teachers, and civil authorities to issue commands where God does not. Not the sole task, to be sure; often enough, parents have to use their authority to enforce such basics as "Don't hit your sister" and county magistrates such fundamentals as "Don't murder your wife." But most parenting is concerned with commands that, while certainly consistent with Scripture, clearly go beyond it: "Clean your room before you come down to breakfast," "Do your math homework before you play with your friends," and so on. The same is true for authorities in school, church, and state. Thus, as Hooker explains, "Those things

---

[16] Richard Hooker, *Of the Laws of Ecclesiastical Polity*, in W. Speed Hill, *The Folger Library Edition of the Works of Richard Hooker, vol. 2: The Laws of Ecclesiastical Polity: Book 5* (Cambridge, MA: Belknap, 1977), 374 [V.71.4]. Spelling and punctuation modernized.

which the Law of God leaveth arbitrary [i.e., unspecified] and at liberty are all subject unto positive laws of men, which laws, for the common benefit, abridge particular men's liberty in such things as far as the rules of equity will suffer. This we must either maintain, or else overturn the world and make every man his own commander."[17]

Indeed, communities (whether churches, schools, cities, etc.) will have no freedom to act *as communities* if they cannot make binding decisions in "matters indifferent"—that is, things that God's moral law neither commands as such nor forbids as such.[18] Corporate liberty can require the limitation of individual liberty. I made this observation in the previous chapter with the example of hymn-singing, but the same of course applies to secular matters as well. Scripture provides no guidance on traffic laws, but any well-governed community must have the authority to make such laws—and compel people to obey them.

That said, compelling people to obey is not the same as "binding consciences"—a crucial distinction too often missed in contemporary evangelical discourse. A close look at Calvin's treatment of the "third part of Christian freedom" can help us wrap our heads around this: "Regarding outward things that are of themselves 'indifferent,' we are not bound before God by any religious obligation preventing us from sometimes using them and other times not using them, indifferently."[19] Calvin

---

[17] Hooker, 374 [V.71.4].

[18] See chaps. 2 and 4 in my *The Peril and Promise of Christian Liberty: Richard Hooker, the Puritans, and Protestant Political Theology* (Grand Rapids, MI: Eerdmans, 2017).

[19] Calvin, *Institutes*, 1:838 [III.19.7].

certainly does not say or intend that we cannot be bound in any sense when it comes to "things indifferent." Rather, we cannot be bound *before God* and *by any religious obligation*. What does this mean? Well, put most simply, it means that human authority cannot compel the conscience because it cannot compel belief; it cannot oblige us to adopt a particular interpretation of the theological status of an action. It can command us *to act*, as long as God has not commanded otherwise, but it cannot command us *to agree* or to think that the command necessarily reflects God's will.

Two examples may be helpful, one from the Reformation period and one from our own.

During the Reformation, one of the biggest battle lines of Christian liberty was over Lent observance. The medieval church had made it binding on conscience to refrain from meat during these forty days; this was generally interpreted as a spiritual requirement, such that to do otherwise was automatically dishonoring to God. Luther, Calvin, and the other Reformers taught otherwise. However, the question then arose whether a civil magistrate might nonetheless continue the ban for other reasons that had nothing to do with salvation. One reason might be to avoid offending the consciences of weaker believers who had not yet grasped the new teaching (much as Paul discusses in 1 Corinthians 8). Or, amusing though it may be to us, they might base such a restriction on the need to protect the fishing industry, which had historically relied on Lent (in which fish had always been permitted as a substitute for meat) for a large portion of its annual sales. It was generally conceded that human authorities could command believers to fast—just not to present the fast as a divine command or something spiritually meritorious. In such a situation, my conscience would remain free to disagree with the rationale for the fast, even as I was still obliged to comply out of respect for authority and public order.

During our own time, perhaps the fiercest battles over Christian liberty concerned mask-wearing and social distancing during the Covid-19 pandemic. Many Christians understandably felt that their consciences were being bound by the command to love their neighbor by wearing a mask—especially if the command extended to include worship services. Of course, few think to protest when church buildings are obliged to conform to fire codes; and even those who might grumble that such codes are too strict would not think of them as Christian liberty violations. And indeed, they are not, any more than a mask ordinance is. Rather, safety regulations take the form of a syllogism: (a) you must love your neighbors by taking reasonable measures to keep them safe; (b) this action is a reasonable measure to keep them safe; ergo (c) you must take this action. A Christian is obliged to believe (a) but *not* (b). But there are reasons to nonetheless *do* (c), even if a Christian does not believe the stated rationale: for instance, out of due respect and honor for God-given leaders or to avoid offending or frightening others. Christians could thus still be asked—and indeed in many cases required—to comply with such policies without any threat to Christian liberty. That is not to justify such policies; there were after all many cogent objections raised to them on many fronts. But however much they may have compromised American Christians' *political liberty*, they were not a threat to their spiritual liberty, except when accompanied (as they sometimes were) by undue guilt-tripping.

We have thus noted three threats to Christian liberty: *legalism*, which consists in a failure to understand the spiritual liberty of the justified sinner; *antinomianism*, which confuses that liberty with a freedom from moral obligation and the law of God; and *anarchism*, which confuses that liberty with a freedom from political obligation and the law of man. Before closing this chapter, I would like to briefly note a fourth threat, or rather, a common mistake that can lead to all three of the dangers just mentioned. This is the mistake of *biblicism*.

For Luther and the Reformers, the proclamation of *sola Scriptura* was closely linked to the proclamation of Christian freedom. It should not be hard to see why, for the late medieval church had oppressed the consciences of believers and mired them in works-righteousness largely by multiplying laws, commandments, and doctrines beyond the text of Scripture. The Reformers sought to set believers free by teaching that God alone could wipe away their sin because only God could declare what *was* sin and what the solution for it was. Article 6 of the Thirty-Nine Articles offered a classic statement of this conviction: "Holy Scripture containeth all things necessary to salvation: so that whatsoever is not read therein, nor may be proved thereby, is not to be required of any man, that it should be believed as an article of the faith, or be thought requisite or necessary to salvation."[20]

This did not mean, however, that Scripture should be understood to contain all things necessary for moral, political, or even

---

[20] "39 Articles of Religion," Church of England, https://www.churchofengland.org/prayer-and-worship/worship-texts-and-resources/book-common-prayer/articles-religion.

ecclesial life. Indeed, on reflection, it is obvious that it cannot; after all, moral and political life consist largely of the sorts of syllogisms noted above. Scripture may provide the major premise (e.g., "love your neighbor as yourself"), but it cannot, generally, supply the minor premise ("in this circumstance, your neighbor needs X"). This, however, has not stopped many Christians, from the Reformation till now, from trying to transform Scripture into a universal rulebook or answer-generator that can solve in advance all the uncertainties of moral and political life.

Such an error leads readily to a new form of legalism, as consciences are weighed down with a host of supposed divine commands that, in some Protestant sects and subcommunities, can make late-medieval Catholicism seem almost liberating by comparison. We have also seen how it might lead to what we have called anarchism, as Richard Hooker worried, by suggesting that, if the Bible hasn't commanded or forbidden something, no one can pass a law about it one way or the other. Paradoxically, it can also engender a certain antinomianism. After all, biblicism can be minimalist as well as maximalist. That is, you might say that "Scripture tells you all you need to know for morality" and "Scripture doesn't actually say a whole lot about morality," thereby concluding that there are only a handful of hard-and-fast moral rules and that, outside these, everything else goes. This style of reasoning is rife within American evangelicalism, which has often read "All things are lawful" in 1 Cor 6:12 and 1 Cor 10:23 as a positive declaration of Pauline teaching, not a libertinism Paul is seeking to undermine.

However free we are in Christ, morality still matters. And morality, although most fully summarized and authoritatively declared in the Old and New Testaments, does not flow out of special revelation alone. The Reformers themselves were well aware of this, noting the manifold ways that pagans, though cut off from salvation, could nonetheless display great outward virtue and moral insight. Calvin, for instance, was deeply taken by the moral teaching of the Stoic philosopher Seneca, and Luther's right-hand man, Philipp Melanchthon, became just the first of many Protestant teachers to write an enthusiastic commentary on Aristotle's *Nicomachean Ethics*.

Accordingly, while we absolutely must begin with spiritual freedom, we cannot end there. Christ liberates us from the curse of sin so that we might then, by the Spirit, progressively grow in freedom from the bondage of our particular sins. Thus, we are enabled to live as free men and women: no longer for ourselves but for Christ and for our neighbors. This experience of striving for freedom from indwelling sin is not unique to Christian believers, even if only they taste the fruits of victory; it is a universal human struggle in which we have much to learn even from the experiences of unbelievers. To this subject of *moral freedom*, then, let us turn in the next chapter.

3

Walking by the Spirit: The Quest for Moral Freedom

> Extreme freedom cannot lead to anything
> but a change to extreme slavery.
> —Plato, *The Republic*

> They promise them freedom, but they
> themselves are slaves of corruption. For whatever
> overcomes a person, to that he is enslaved.
> —2 Peter 2:19

> O God, who art the author of peace and lover
> of concord, in knowledge of whom standeth our
> eternal life, whose service is perfect freedom.
> —Thomas Cranmer, The Book of Common Prayer

Living as Free People

The spiritual liberty that Martin Luther proclaimed, and the apostle Paul before him, was an all-or-nothing thing: we *have been* set free by Christ, and all that remains is for us to confidently lay hold of this proclamation and experience the peace that comes from the banishing of all fear. As the answer to the first question of the Heidelberg Catechism puts it, "Because I belong to him, Christ, by his Holy Spirit, assures me of eternal life, and makes me wholeheartedly willing and ready from now on to live for him."[1] Luther's Roman Catholic opponents could not make sense of this confidence, seeing it as mere presumption. After all, are not each of us in this life constantly weighed down by sinful desires and constantly prone to act on them in ways that belie our status as one of the redeemed?

The Reformers, however, were well aware of this tension. As liberating as the free gift of forgiveness is, casting off the burden of fear and transforming us from slaves to sons and daughters, it is only a beginning. "The entire life of the faithful," as Luther wrote in his *Ninety-Five Theses*, must "be one of penitence,"[2] a constant struggle against the bondage of indwelling sin. Unlike their Roman Catholic opponents, however, the Reformers explained this struggle as something fundamentally different from the once-for-all gift of spiritual freedom purchased by the blood of Christ. That spiritual freedom was the effect of justification, rendering possible the pursuit of moral freedom with the aid of the Spirit, which they called

---

[1] The Heidelberg Catechism (1563), Q. 1, Reformed Church of America, https://www.rca.org/about/theology/creeds-and-confessions/the-heidelberg-catechism/.

[2] Martin Luther, *Martin Luther's 95 Theses, with Introduction, Commentary, and Study Guide*, ed. and trans. Timothy J. Wengert (Minneapolis: Fortress, 2015). 13.

sanctification. By justification we are freed all at once from bondage to the accusing voice of the law. By sanctification we are freed little by little from the bondage to indwelling sin, with the law now transformed from cruel taskmaster to loving guide, aiding us in our struggle.

Scripture itself speaks clearly both about the reality of such moral struggle and about the necessity for Christians to engage in it. Though we might already have the *status* of free men and women, we must seek to bring our lives into conformity with this status: "Live as people who are free," Peter exhorts us (1 Pet 2:16). And what does it mean to live as those who are free? Paradoxically, it means to give up that freedom, sacrificing oneself as the "dutiful servant of all," as Luther puts it. And as we noted above, Luther is simply following the logic of Paul in Galatians 5: "For you were called to freedom, brothers. Only do not use your freedom as an opportunity for the flesh, but through love serve one another" (v. 13). To bring ourselves into subjection to others, we must first bring our evil desires into subjection to the Spirit: "But I say, walk by the Spirit, and you will not gratify the desires of the flesh. For the desires of the flesh are against the Spirit, and the desires of the Spirit are against the flesh, for these are opposed to each other, to keep you from doing the things you want to do" (Gal 5:16–17).

This, as every Christian knows, is a bitter and lifelong battle, one that Paul describes vividly in the text from Romans 7 with which we began this book:

> For I have the desire to do what is right, but not the ability to carry it out. For I do not do the good I want, but the evil I do not want is what I keep on doing. . . .

> For I delight in the law of God, in my inner being, but I see in my members another law waging war against the law of my mind and making me captive to the law of sin that dwells in my members. (Rom 7:18–19, 22–23)

Although in regeneration we have received a new heart that earnestly loves God and desires to please him, this "new self" coexists with an "old self" that is still "corrupt through deceitful desires" (Eph 4:22), so we must labor day by day to put the old self to death, a process that Protestant theologians used to refer to as "mortification." As Zacharias Ursinus writes in the *Commentary to the Heidelberg Catechism*, "The mortification of the old man, or of the flesh, consists in the laying off and subduing of the corruption of our nature."[3] Our sin nature is like a deadly serpent coiled tight around the new heart we have received in Christ, seeking to strangle us; we must hack at it with all our might if we are to enjoy the full freedom of the children of God—a moral as well as a spiritual freedom.

This moral freedom consists, as C. S. Lewis observed in *The Abolition of Man*, in restoring the right relation between three aspects of man's nature: the head, the chest, and the belly—that is, the reason, the "spirited emotions," and the bodily appetites. If these are not in harmony—the head ruling the belly through the assistance of the chest, then we will find that we keep on doing the evil we do not want.[4] In saying this, however, Lewis

---

[3] Zacharias Ursinus, *Commentary on the Heidelberg Catechism* (1585) in *Reformation Theology: A Reader of Primary Sources with Introductions*, ed. W. Bradford Littlejohn and Jonathan Roberts (Moscow, ID: Davenant, 2017), 514.

[4] C. S. Lewis, *The Abolition of Man* (New York: Macmillan, 1960), chap. 1.

was not summarizing something unique to the Christian moral tradition, but rather he was reviewing ideas originally wrestled through by pagan Greeks and Romans. Let us take a few pages to survey their insights before pointing to their completion (and transformation) by the Christian gospel.

The Pagan Search for Self-Mastery

This struggle to attain moral freedom, of course, is not unique to Christians. No human being is a stranger to the experience of moral struggle, the attempt to follow the "better angels of our nature"[5] and overcome the base desires dragging us earthward. While all such struggle is doomed to failure outside of Christ, we should not lightly despise it. For one thing, the unbeliever who triumphs over his worst impulses and tries to heed the voice of conscience, which still whispers in every ear (Rom 2:14–15), will be a much better neighbor and a much better citizen than one who runs headlong in pursuit of every appetite. For another, those who have bent their minds earnestly upon this struggle have often gained profound insight into human nature and have a great deal to teach us as Christians. Indeed, the greatest Christian moral thinkers through the ages have usually taken as their starting point the ideas of virtue developed by Greek and Roman thinkers questing after moral freedom.

Plato understood, as did Paul, the reality of moral conflict between "the flesh" and "the mind"—that frequently we find ourselves *wanting* to do things that we *know* we shouldn't do.[6] This can be as trivial as indulging in a decadent bowl of ice

---

[5] Abraham Lincoln, First Inaugural Address, March 1861.

[6] In an early dialogue, the *Meno*, Plato treats moral failure as the result of intellectual error, suggesting that those who truly *know* what

cream or as serious as seducing a neighbor's spouse, but whether the stakes are great or small and whether the battle is long or short, every day we experience this internal battle. *Rationally*, we know better, but *emotionally*, sometimes we want something so badly that we don't care about the consequences; or worse yet, our desires co-opt our reason and give us "rationalizations" so that we can pretend to ourselves that we are acting thoughtfully and responsibly.

Plato introduced the notion of the three "levels" to the soul: the reason, the "spirited emotions," and the appetites.[7] After all, not all emotions are created equal: the love of honor is not on the same plane as the love of alcohol, and frequently the former can be deployed to restrain the latter. Indeed, such higher emotions are often much more effective than mere reason in holding us back from our worst impulses. But even the loftiest emotions can get out of hand: a love of honor, for instance, may manifest not merely as courage but as foolhardy rashness—thus do many of the characters in Homer's *Iliad* meet untimely ends. The highest virtue then, justice, establishes a proper hierarchy and harmony between the different levels of each man's soul. According to Plato:

> "[Justice] means that he does not allow the elements in him each to do the job of some other, or the three sorts

---

is good for them will surely do it. But in his later dialogues, he offers a richer moral psychology that recognizes the reality of internal strife.

[7] Plato, *Republic*, trans. C. D. C Reeve (Indianapolis: Hackett, 2004), bk. 4. See also his metaphor of the chariot in the *Phaedrus*, where the intellect serves as a charioteer trying to steer the soul heavenward, as two horses pull it: one, representing the passions, constantly pulls it earthward; the other, representing *thumos* or "the spirited emotions," works with the charioteer to resist the passions.

of elements in his soul to meddle with one another. Instead, he regulates well what is really his own, rules himself, puts himself in order, becomes his own friend, and harmonizes the three elements together."[8]

Plato recognized that those accustomed to give free rein to their appetites will think of such justice as the loss of freedom (both at the individual level and at the political level), but they fail to realize that the "freedom" of following one's appetites is simply the road to slavery. Such a man "lives from day to day, gratifying the appetite of the moment.... There is neither order nor necessity in his life, yet he calls it pleasant, free, and blessedly happy, and follows it throughout his entire life."[9] He revolts against any imposition of order and "take[s] no notice of the laws—written or unwritten—in order to avoid having any master at all."[10] But what he fails to realize is that "extreme freedom cannot lead to anything but a change to extreme slavery, whether in a private individual or a city."[11] In such a city, someone will arise from among the people and, by demagoguery, rally them to his support, until he has established himself as a tyrant among them. In an individual, one desire, indulged over and over, will eventually gain mastery over the whole person in that bondage we call addiction. Indeed, the tyrant, drunk on power, will himself soon be tyrannized by his own desires: "Mustn't his soul be full of slavery and illiberality, with those same parts of it enslaved, while a small part, the most wicked and insane, is

---

[8] Plato, *Republic*, 132 [IV, 443d].
[9] Plato, 259 [VIII, 561c-d].
[10] Plato, 261 [VIII, 563d-e].
[11] Plato, 262 [VIII, 564a].

master?"[12] Plato concluded, in words reminiscent of Paul's in Romans 1, "So, a tyrannical soul will also least do what it wishes . . . and will be full of disorder and regret."[13] The just man, then, is he who "rules himself." The man who, determined to be free, casts off every rule, ends up being ruled by his worst impulses, those that least represent his true self.

Plato's disciple Aristotle refined many of these insights in his *Nicomachean Ethics*. If the man enslaved to his desires is deeply unhappy and if desire is driven by the sense of lack, then it follows, argued Aristotle, that the happy soul is one that is "self-sufficient . . . lacking in nothing"[14] and thus wholly master of its desires. This self-mastery required above all the virtues of courage and temperance—courage to steel us against overbearing fear of pain and temperance to arm us against overbearing love of pleasure. Cicero would later summarize, "Supplement it [courage] with self-control—the power to keep every emotion in check—and then every ingredient you could need for the happy life is yours. For you will have courage as your defence against distress and fear, and self-control to liberate you from sensuality and keep you free of immoderate ravings."[15]

While for Aristotle and Cicero "self-sufficiency" did not mean the negation of desire but, rather, the proper balancing of desires so that each served only the true needs of the soul, many of the Stoics influenced by them began to ask whether the

---

[12] Plato, 277 [IX, 577d].

[13] Plato, 277 [IX, 577e].

[14] Aristotle, *Nicomachean Ethics*, trans. W. D. Ross in *The Basic Works of Aristotle*, ed. Richard McKeon (New York: Modern Library, 2001), 942 [I, 1097b].

[15] Cicero, *On the Good Life*, ed. Michael Grant (New York: Penguin, 1971), 75.

simplest and truest route to authentic freedom, and therefore happiness, was not the transcendence of all desire. The Stoics saw freedom as independence—the truly free soul was its own master by needing no one and nothing else for its happiness. So, Epictetus would write in the second century AD, "Art thou then free? a man may say. So help me heaven, I long and pray for freedom! But I cannot look my masters boldly in the face; I still value the poor body; I still set much store on its preservation whole and sound."[16] The true picture of a free man, asserted Epictetus, was the legendary Diogenes the Cynic, who lived in a tub, without possessions or clothes: "He had cast away every handle whereby slavery might lay hold upon him, nor was it possible for any to approach and take hold of him to enslave him. All things sat loose upon him—all things were to him attached by but slender ties."[17]

Such Stoic freedom, achieving self-mastery by self-transcendence, subordinating every desire to the sense of duty, has held a powerful attraction in every age. Even in the late eighteenth century, the philosopher Immanuel Kant would articulate a similar theory of freedom. Freedom, he insisted, lay in autonomy, which literally means being a "law to oneself." But he did not mean this in the colloquial sense of doing whatever one wanted. Quite the opposite—rejecting all concrete wants and desires, even, he insisted, the desire to benefit others, the free soul observed the law laid down by reason alone, out of

---

[16] Epictetus, *The Stoic Path: The Golden Sayings*, trans. Hastings Crossley (New York: St. Martin's, 2022), 1.141.

[17] Epictetus, *The Golden Sayings of Epictetus*, trans. Hastings Crossley, Harvard Classics, vol. 2 (New York: P. F. Collier and Sons, 1937), 168.

pure duty and nothing else. Even to think in terms of reward or punishment as incentives to action, Kant argued, was to compromise the perfect self-sufficiency of the rational soul.[18]

Long before Kant, however, the Christian philosopher Boethius, himself deeply shaped by the Stoic tradition, had pricked the bubble of such idolatrous self-sufficiency in his masterpiece dialogue, *The Consolation of Philosophy*. After going through the various potential sources of earthly happiness one by one, Lady Philosophy concludes, "Clearly, therefore, these things offer man only shadows of the true good, or imperfect blessings, and cannot confer true and perfect good."[19] The only truly self-sufficient being, she demonstrates, can be God himself; and human happiness, then, is only possible through participation in and union with God: "Since happiness is in fact divinity, it is clear that it is through the possession of divinity that they become happy."[20]

Receiving Ourselves from Outside Ourselves: Moral Freedom through the Spirit

Since for Boethius and the tradition he represents, "happiness" is essentially identical with what we have called "moral freedom," we can see that the struggle for self-mastery that

---

[18] Immanuel Kant, *Groundwork to the Metaphysics of Morals*, trans. and ed. Mary Gregor and Jens Timmermann (Cambridge: Cambridge University Press, 1998).

[19] Boethius, *The Consolation of Philosophy*, trans. V. E. Watts (London: The Folio Society, 1998), 102 [III.9].

[20] Boethius, 106 [III.10].

constituted the highest pagan ideal of freedom turns out to be a dead end. Whereas Plato and those who followed him tended to think of (1) fleshly desires as the main threat to freedom and (2) the right exercise of reason as the ticket to true freedom, the apostle Paul's understanding of human bondage to sin was much more radical. While he spoke of the battle against "the flesh," it is clear that the term encompasses not merely the baser appetites but the whole old self. As Luther, who understood this more clearly than most before him, wrote in his preface to the book of Romans, "Thou must not understand 'flesh,' therefore, as though that only were 'flesh' which is connected with unchastity, but St. Paul uses 'flesh' of the whole man, body, and soul, reason, and all his faculties included, because all that is in him longs and strives after the flesh."[21]

In this, Luther was channeling Augustine, who a millennium before had unmasked the futility of pagan virtue. Even in its best forms, such virtue consisted merely in using one form of self-love (pride) to hold in check a lower form of self-love. Even in their finest moments of self-transcendence, the philosophers remained, in Augustine's memorable phrase, *incurvatus in se* (curved in upon themselves) and thus unable to experience the true moral freedom that consists in living as we are truly meant to live: for others. Such authentic moral freedom is made possible only by first experiencing the spiritual freedom we have described in the last chapter: "[Christ] died for all, that those who live might no longer live for themselves but for him who for their sake died and was raised" (2 Cor 5:15). If the whole man

---

[21] Martin Luther, *Preface to the Letter of St. Paul to the Romans*, trans. Andrew Thornton, https://www.ccel.org/l/luther/romans/pref_romans.html.

is flesh, if the whole man lies in bondage under sin, then the only escape from bondage must come from outside. As Oliver O'Donovan beautifully puts it in his *Desire of the Nations*:

> There is no freedom except when what we are, and do, corresponds to what has been given to us to be and to do. "Given to us," because the law of our being does assert itself spontaneously merely by virtue of our existing. We must receive ourselves from outside ourselves, addressed by a summons which evokes that correspondence of existence to being. "Where the Spirit of the Lord is, there is liberty" (2 Cor. 3:[17]).[22]

This dependence on the Spirit is a lifelong one. We must resist the temptation to think of justification by faith as a prerequisite for a sanctification by works, as if we first receive forgiveness by grace and then gain mastery over sin by the sheer force of our wills. No, as the Reformers emphasized, the mortification of sin in the life of the believer requires a constant dependence on the Spirit, the source of our new life and true freedom: "It is God who works in you, both to will and to work for his good pleasure" (Phil 2:13). As the Heidelberg Catechism puts it in answer to the question, "Why then should we do good works?": "Because Christ, having redeemed us by his blood, is also restoring us by his Spirit into his image."[23]

---

[22] Oliver O'Donovan, *The Desire of the Nations: Rediscovering the Roots of Political Theology* (Cambridge: Cambridge University Press, 1996), 252.

[23] The Heidelberg Catechism (1563), Q. 86, Reformed Church of America, https://www.rca.org/about/theology/creeds-and-confessions/the-heidelberg-catechism/.

As we walk by the Spirit and seek to mortify the deeds of the flesh, we will come to realize how impotent even our higher faculties of reason and will can be, and we will call out instead for divine assistance to break the chains that still hold us in slavery. There is a memorable scene in C. S. Lewis's *Great Divorce*, in which a soul, struggling with bondage to lust, cannot argue his way out of the temptation and instead must humble himself to accept the aid of an angel who offers to slay the creature (that is, the disordered part of his own soul) that is tormenting him.[24] To be truly free, we must receive ourselves from outside ourselves.

Learning from the Pagans

All of that said, we should not be hasty in dismissing the insights of the pagan quest for moral freedom. While sometimes the Spirit does act suddenly and decisively to break the bonds of some besetting sin in our lives, more often the Spirit works by creaturely means and expects us to make use of these means ourselves. A man who sits passively around waiting on God to give him victory over temptation is just as deluded as one who thinks that he can gain full victory by his own resources. For this reason, Christian moral theologians throughout the centuries have drawn heavily on the insights of Plato, Aristotle, Cicero, and Epictetus in formulating an understanding of *the virtues*—habits of soul and body by which we more and more grow to instinctively shun what is evil and pursue what is good.

---

[24] C. S. Lewis, *The Great Divorce* (New York: HarperCollins, 2001), 106–12.

Whatever the limitations of the Platonic theory of the three-tiered soul, it still rings basically true two and a half millennia later, as Lewis so persuasively argues in chapter 1 of *The Abolition of Man*. There really is a hierarchy of impulses and desires, beginning with those we share with the lowest beasts (such as food and sex), ascending to those we seem to share only with the noblest creatures (such as shame and honor), and finally reaching those unique to us as human beings (the exercise of reason and rational deliberation). And while, as embodied creatures, we should not reject or ignore the lower bodily desires, we should use our higher faculties to hold them in check, not allowing ourselves to be mastered by any one desire.

Moreover, although the Stoics might have taken their ideal of self-sufficiency to an extreme, there was a profound insight in their insistence that we will never be happy if we find our happiness in things that lie beyond our control. The Stoics were among the first to explore the distinction between *inward freedom* and *outward freedom*, observing that every form of outward freedom is contingent and unstable. As the apostle James observed, "Come now, you who say, 'Today or tomorrow we will go into such and such a town and spend a year there and trade and make a profit'—yet you do not know what tomorrow will bring. What is your life? For you are a mist that appears for a little time and then vanishes" (Jas 4:13–14). According to the Stoics, freedom that depends on circumstances is vain and empty; true freedom will be found in detachment and true contentment. Of course, the Stoics failed to realize that this is only possible by not retreating to the inner citadel of one's mind but by resting on Christ.

The Search for Authenticity

The ancient philosophers, like we moderns, were on a quest for authentic selfhood, but though they went astray in their quest, they were much nearer the mark than the libertinism of our modern age. We are still, as much as ever, in search of our "true selves," but our ideas of what this means have transformed radically, and along with these changed notions, our ideal of freedom has also changed.

Today, authenticity is sought in "self-expression," with social media providing an unprecedented vehicle for each individual to express and represent his or her true self, his or her individuality. Never mind that most social media performances follow predictable and well-worn scripts and pander shamelessly to the likes and reactions of the crowd. Everyone manages to imagine that on their TikTok or Instagram accounts, they have found a space where they can finally "be me," defying the demands of parents, peers, or imagined oppressive forces. To "be me" means above all to be uninhibited, to give free rein to my thoughts and desires, to "let it all hang out." In this new philosophy of freedom, restraint has become "repression," and taboos exist to be violated. All the moral and social norms that were once thought to foster healthy self-control are seen as simply attempts by society to control me and keep me from being myself.

In the new moral order, the classic hierarchy of the soul has been inverted. The bodily appetites, far from needing to be held in check by a sense of honor and shame and, above all, by reason, ought to be indulged, for they represent my true authentic self. We are encouraged to "get in touch with our feelings" and, having done so, to "do what feels right." Of course, the most powerful feelings of all are those driven by physical desires, and sexual desire above all. Thus, whereas Plato, Boethius, and the whole Christian tradition warned of the folly of seeking happiness in something so fleeting as physical pleasure, the apostles of the new morality openly promote it. "If happiness be the object of morality . . . if the worthiness of any action is to be estimated by the quantity of pleasurable sensation it is calculated to produce, then the connection of the sexes is so long sacred as it contributes to the comfort of the parties," wrote the romantic poet Percy Bysshe Shelley.[25] Accordingly, as Carl Trueman has powerfully analyzed in his *Rise and Triumph of the Modern Self*, sexual freedom has become the paradigmatic form of freedom and self-expression in the modern world. Any restraint on sexual freedom—even the mere registering of personal disapproval of some sexual act—is increasingly taken as an intolerable violation of selfhood.

If freedom is seen as independence and autonomy, there is a paradox here, of course, for sexuality is above all a marker of our dependence and interdependence. The sexual union requires the coming together of two human beings, and its natural fruit is the creation of a new human being, a "dependent" with a permanent claim on its parents, however much they may seek to disown it. Our sexuality is a reminder of our own natality, the fact that each of us is not in fact self-sufficient but radically dependent on those who begat, bore, and raised us. Hence the

---

[25] Percy Bysshe Shelley, *Poetical Works*, ed. Thomas Hutchinson, corr. G. M. Matthews (Oxford: Oxford University Press, 1971), 806, quoted in Carl R. Trueman, *The Rise and Triumph of the Modern Self: Cultural Amnesia, Expressive Individualism, and the Road to Sexual Revolution* (Wheaton, IL: Crossway, 2020), 153.

fervor with which the modern world has been at work to destroy the link between sexuality and natality, first with contraception and then with abortion. If God created sexuality as a reminder of our limits, of our radical dependence on one another and the ties that bind each generation to the next, it is no wonder that abortion has become the virtual sacrament of the progressive religion, asserting our godlike freedom in a gesture of defiance of all such limits.

Of course, even this is not enough to satisfy the self-absorbed modern ideal of freedom, for traditionally, sex still depends upon another, finding its fulfillment in yielding to what is radically other than myself. No wonder then that the sexual revolution has progressed so rapidly from the ideal of "free love" (in which an individual man and woman sought pleasure in a fleeting no-strings-attached union), to homosexual love (in which a man or woman seeks pleasure not in one who is "other" but in a mirror of his or her own self), to self-love, as seen in the now-ubiquitous cult of masturbation and pornography. Of course, we all know deep down what a lie this is—for the only form of bondage more degrading than the bondage the pornography addict inflicts on the bodies he exploits is the bondage he inflicts upon himself.

We are beset today with the false prophets of which the apostle Peter warned two millennia ago:

> These are waterless springs and mists driven by a storm. For them the gloom of utter darkness has been reserved. For, speaking loud boasts of folly, they entice by sensual passions of the flesh those who are barely escaping from those who live in error. They promise them freedom, but they themselves are slaves of

corruption. For whatever overcomes a person, to that he is enslaved. (2 Pet 2:17–19)

The Roots of Modern Bondage

Our societal descent into the dark abyss of this self-enslavement called "freedom" has been remarkably swift, commencing in the Enlightenment's declaration of man's "release from his self-incurred tutelage"[26] and ending in a society slack-jawed before our ever-flickering screens. Interestingly, while this project began with Plato's "head" enjoining us to "dare to think for yourself," it soon slid down into the "chest" with the maxim "follow your heart," before coming to rest in the belly: "do what feels right." Why? How did a project that began with the enthronement of reason end in the abandonment of it?

Aristotle would have had little trouble explaining it: man is a "political animal," as he famously remarked, and although good laws depend on good morals, good morals also depend on good laws—a circular relationship that Plato explored at length in his *Republic*. Individual freedom, in other words, cannot survive on the foundation of individualism. In *Rise and Triumph of the Modern Self*, Carl Trueman quotes an instructive passage from the French Enlightenment philosopher Jean-Jacques Rousseau, who was perhaps responsible more than anyone else for the rise of the modern cult of authenticity. Rousseau, unlike the nihilistic libertines of TikTok today, believed "the eternal laws of nature and order do exist," but unlike his predecessors, he

---

[26] Immanuel Kant, "What Is Enlightenment?" (1784), *Modern History Sourcebook*, https://sourcebooks.fordham.edu/mod/kant-whatis.asp.

believed they could replace political order: "For the wise man, they take the place of positive law." The wise man, then, should ignore the laws and customs of his own community and follow only the law within: "It is to these [laws of conscience] that he ought to enslave himself in order to be free.... Freedom is found in no form of government; it is in the heart of the free man. He takes it with him everywhere."[27]

But of course, as the ancients and the Christian tradition knew well, freedom requires government, what James called "the perfect law ... of liberty" (Jas 1:25), without which none of us will ever learn the discipline by which we can transcend our desires. Every culture, as Trueman observed, had its "therapists" (usually priests and religious leaders) to help individuals whose souls were in tumult find rest and freedom in conformity to the norms by which they might govern their passions: "Traditionally, the role of the therapist in any given culture was to enable the patient to grasp the nature of the community to which he belonged."[28] Now, however, notes Trueman, the role has been inverted, and the therapist "seeks to protect the individual from the kind of harmful neuroses that society creates through its smothering of the individual's ability simply to be herself."[29] Rather than social and political structures providing a stable context within which an individual could find meaning and therefore freedom by conforming, these structures themselves are now asked to conform to the whims of the

---

[27] Jean-Jacques Rousseau, *Emile; or, On Education*, trans. Allan Bloom (New York: Basic Books, 1979), 473, in Trueman, *Rise and Triumph*, 124.

[28] Trueman, *Rise and Triumph*, 47.

[29] Trueman, 48.

individual—quite literally so, as in the redesigning of physical structures to include transgender bathrooms: "Outward institutions [have] become in effect the servants of the individual and her sense of inner well-being."[30]

The loss of moral freedom, then, cannot be explained merely in theological terms. Although *spiritual freedom* may provide the unshakeable foundation for any ultimately stable moral freedom, the walls and pillars are made of laws. Moral freedom will be unsuitable without a proper understanding and practice of *political freedom*, the third member of our triad. Indeed, there is a reciprocal relationship, for moral freedom is at once the prerequisite of political freedom (a free government, as America's Founders well understood, depends on a virtuous people) and also the fruit of it. A healthy society of healthy individuals will depend on a positive feedback loop of free people and free laws, while a decadent society is one in which the feedback loop has gone into reverse, with slavish people creating and demanding ever more slavish institutions, which in turn feed worse and worse forms of moral bondage. Such is our crisis of civilization today. To find our way out of it, a revival of faith alone will not suffice; we also need a renewal of political imagination.

---

[30] Trueman, 49.

4

Between Right and Rights: Making Sense of Political Freedom

> In those days there was no king in Israel. Everyone did what was right in his own eyes.
> —Judges 21:25

> I know not what course others may take; but as for me, give me liberty or give me death!
> —Patrick Henry (1775)

> It is time for our people to distinguish more accurately than they seem to do between liberty and licentiousness. The late revolution would lose much of its glory, as well as utility, if our conduct should confirm the tory maxim, "That men are incapable of governing themselves."
> —John Jay (1786)

Freedom and the Pursuit of Happiness

As we turn our attention to political freedom, we might be tempted to emit a sigh of relief, for now at least we are back on familiar territory. "Freedom" is the universal language of contemporary politics, especially in modern America. Indeed, Americans are almost tempted to believe that they invented it because theirs was the first nation to build its constitution on the ideal of freedom, a luminous example of liberty to all the other nations of the earth. It is right there in our Declaration of Independence, where we proclaimed the "self-evident" truth that the Creator had endowed every people with the rights to "life, liberty, and the pursuit of happiness" and that the sole purpose of government was to secure such rights. But much depends on how we understand such "rights" and such "happiness." Is happiness a subjective feeling, produced by a set of personal preferences that differ from one person to another? Or is it something more holistic and objective, rooted in human nature and perfected by virtue, that the ancients called *eudaimonia*? If the former, then the task of government is to secure individual *rights* in the plural, a sphere within which we demand to be left alone, free to set and pursue our own purposes. If the latter, then it seems the task of government will include the use of laws to protect and promote a life of virtue, ordered toward *right* (in the singular).[1] Within the politics of *rights*, political

---

[1] To be clear, the distinction between plural *rights* and singular *right* is an oversimplification, and it is quite possible to talk about individual rights from within a moral and political vision committed to a singular objective ideal of *the* right. The question, however, is which concept provides the starting point. See Oliver O'Donovan, "The Language of Rights and Conceptual History," *Journal of Religious*

freedom has little to do with the moral freedom we've just discussed in the last chapter; but within the politics of *right*, in which constraint and freedom are not opposed, the two will be closely connected.

From the former standpoint (rights), which dominates our world today, the liberty to pursue happiness must necessarily be as flexible and open-ended as possible. It is the liberty of a wide-open playing field stocked with recreational supplies of every description and cans of spray paint so that each participant can mark out his own lines and goals as the whim takes him. A government tasked with upholding such liberty will find itself in the position of a referee called upon to manage a baseball game, a football game, and a soccer match simultaneously—with a few golfers thrown in for good measure. No wonder our contemporary politics feels like chaos! From the latter standpoint (right), however, political freedom will be more like the freedom that a well-coached football team enjoys: the freedom to run an amazing touchdown play not only by practicing excellence within the rules of the game but also by submitting to the guidance of the coach and quarterback. A team on which every player was free to pursue his own purposes would be a team free only to lose!

The shift from the older politics of right to the newer politics of rights—often called political liberalism—is well summarized in a famous passage from Thomas Jefferson's *Notes on the State of Virginia*: "The legitimate powers of government extend to such acts only as are injurious to others. But it does me no injury for my neighbor to say there are twenty gods, or no god.

Ethics 37, no. 2 (2009): 193–207; Nigel Biggar, *What's Wrong with Rights?* (Oxford: Oxford University Press, 2020).

It neither picks my pocket nor breaks my leg."[2] Here, in one fell swoop, Jefferson pulls the rug out from under what had historically been one of the central concerns of politics, including among the Protestant Reformers: protecting and promoting the right worship of God. After all, if to serve him is perfect freedom, as Christianity had long taught,[3] then political freedom is inseparable from right religion. Indeed, if the purpose of politics is to promote happiness, how can a people be happy without God? "Our hearts are restless until we rest in him," wrote Augustine.[4] Perhaps, perhaps not, replied Jefferson: but government's concern is with the body, not the soul; and as long as bad doctrine does no harm to the body of my neighbor, it is of no political concern.[5]

We will have more to say about religious liberty in particular when we come to chapter 7, but for now it highlights a tension. On the one hand, Jefferson's breezy dismissal of the consequences of false religion cannot be right; on the other hand, today we instinctively shy away from the idea of the government forcing us to worship rightly. If a politics of rights seems too

---

[2] Thomas Jefferson, "Notes on the State of Virginia, Query XVII," in *Jefferson: Political Writings*, ed. Joyce Appleby and Terence Ball (Cambridge: Cambridge University Press, 1999), 394.

[3] "O GOD who art the author of peace and lover of concord, . . . whose service is perfect freedom . . ." "Morning Prayer: A Collect for Peace," Church of England, https://www.churchofengland.org/prayer-and-worship/worship-texts-and-resources/book-common-prayer/order-morning-prayer.

[4] Augustine, *Confessions*, trans. J. G. Pilkington, in *Nicene and Post-Nicene Fathers, First Series*, ed. Philip Schaff, vol. 1 (Buffalo: Christian Literature, 1887), I.1.1, https://www.newadvent.org/fathers/110101.htm.

[5] See Jefferson, "Notes on the State of Virginia, Query XVII."

anarchic, a politics of right may seem too authoritarian. That is why a full account of political freedom must incorporate elements of each—rights and right—into a synthesis built on the idea of self-government through law. In this chapter, we will begin with a high-level historical survey of the development of a modern liberal politics of rights from an ancient politics of right. Then we will consider the nuanced vision of political liberty that guided most of the American Founders and that is worth recovering today.

A Liberty of Political Right

Traditional societies, rather than prizing freedom of choice as an intrinsic good, were much more interested in *what* people chose and in providing them the context, constraints, and incentives to enable them to choose well. These constraints generally took the form of classes or stations within society, within which individuals found their proper place and knew what was expected of them. The liberty they pursued was a positive liberty, a capacity to engage in meaningful action based on shared norms, and it was for the most part a communal liberty, in which the community as a whole worked together toward a common good and a common happiness.

Such a society might sound deeply attractive or downright alarming, depending on your predispositions. Indeed, it can be both. On the one hand, it holds the assurance of offering a meaning to life that most often escapes the aimless and rootless modern. It sees freedom not as something found where politics ends, something discovered in the play of private life, but rather as "exclusively located in the political realm," as Hannah

Arendt, one of the shrewdest analysts of this ancient freedom, observes.[6] It was only by participating together in political life, in the shared business of the *polis* rather than in private pursuits driven by appetite or necessity, that men (and for the Greeks it was indeed only men) could experience freedom. Such freedom called for a comprehensive dedication to something greater than the individual, a *res publica* (literally, "public thing") that alone promised the immortality for which every man longs but which earthly life otherwise seems unable to offer. Within this public, and the clear hierarchy of values it provided, the free man could speak great words and do great deeds, confident that their value would be recognized not only by his fellows then alive but by all posterity. So declared Pericles in his famous funeral oration during the Peloponnesian War: "For this offering of their lives, made in common by them all, they each of them individually received that renown which never grows old, and for a tomb, not so much that in which their bones have been deposited, but that noblest of shrines wherein their glory is laid up to be eternally remembered upon every occasion on which deed or story shall be commemorated."[7]

An attractive prospect, to be sure, but it had its darker side, as the early Christians were quick to point out. For one, it made an idol out of the *polis*, demanding from the city of man what only the city of God could offer, and promising an

---

[6] Hannah Arendt, *The Human Condition*, 2nd ed., with an introduction by Margaret Canovan (Chicago: University of Chicago Press, 1998), 31.

[7] Robert B. Strassler, ed., *The Landmark Thucydides: A Comprehensive Guide to The Peloponnesian War* (New York: Touchstone, 1998), 115.

immortality that it could not in the end deliver. As Boethius noted in his *Consolation of Philosophy*, even the most famous man at any given time will be forgotten by most of the human race.[8] For another, this shared public may have made freedom possible *inside* its bounds, but it required an *outside*—an outside composed of women, slaves, and barbarians. All of these were consigned by either nature or fate to a life of necessity, rather than freedom, and were thus fit to be exploited by those fortunate enough to be called to freedom. Nowhere was the early church more subversive than in its determination to lift up these scattered outcasts and incorporate them into a cosmopolitan community that gave freedom to all. This positive freedom of the ancient *polis* also had a natural bent toward totalitarianism. If, after all, an Athenian or Spartan or Roman could confidently define the "good" for mankind and say what happiness looked like, and if such happiness could only be achieved by the common striving of all, then the laws of the city could not afford to leave a freeman free to his own devices or to form his own purposes.

Christianity shattered the idolatry of the ancient *polis* but did not thereby usher in an era of individual freedom as we think of it today. It, too, taking for granted that God's "service is perfect freedom,"[9] that human beings find their happiness in obedience to God, and that each of us has been born into a particular station by God's good providence, tended to see no contradiction between the proclamation of Christian liberty and the demands of political order. This was true even for

---

[8] Boethius, *The Consolation of Philosophy*, trans. V. E. Watts (London: The Folio Society, 1998), III.6.

[9] "Morning Prayer: A Collect for Peace."

the Protestant Reformation, often maligned (or celebrated) as marking the end of authority and the triumph of individualism. Indeed, the Reformers still believed emphatically that sinful individuals were notoriously poor judges of what would make them and those around them happy; furthermore, they believed that society should be knit together as closely as possible by shared norms guiding each political community toward its common good. Luther's "here I stand" was not meant to be a blueprint for everyday politics, for which Luther rather preached the call to submission (Romans 13) as the general rule.

However, Christianity—and especially the Reformation—did render the world a crucial service by reminding earthly rulers that there lay a domain of human life far beyond their competence to command. Each citizen was made not merely to be an obedient subject but was possessed of an immortal soul that stood accountable to God alone and was ultimately freed from bondage to earthly norms or fear of earthly punishments because that soul served a higher lord. By means of this truth the bounds of political power were slowly but steadily rolled back. Freedom now could be found not merely within the practice of politics but also beyond it in the life of the heart and the mind and in the shared life of a Christian community bound by love rather than law.[10] Such was the stirring implication of Luther's clarion call in *The Freedom of a Christian*.

---

[10] See Oliver O'Donovan, *The Desire of the Nations: Rediscovering the Roots of Political Theology* (Cambridge: Cambridge University Press, 1996), 255; W. Bradford Littlejohn, *The Peril and Promise of Christian Liberty: Richard Hooker, the Puritans, and Protestant Political Theology* (Grand Rapids: Eerdmans, 2017), chap. 7.

Indeed, the Reformation helped open the doors to a new conception of liberty not only by its teaching on conscience but also indirectly by its stress on the importance of education and literacy. A society within which everyone was encouraged to read the Word of God for himself or herself, weighing the deepest questions of human existence within his or her own soul, was a society in which citizens would begin to ask more questions of their rulers and demand more avenues to have their perspectives and interests represented. It was also a society in which different visions of God's will had more space to proliferate, as Protestants read the Scriptures, listened to sermons, and debated divergent theories of church government or worship practices. In response to such debates, Protestant political thinkers felt the need to start rethinking the boundaries of political liberty.

A Liberty of Political Rights

This rethinking, pursued over several centuries, led to the emergence of what we today call liberalism—a political philosophy dedicated to limited government and promotion of individual freedom. This vision emerged out of the Reformation's gradual rethinking of religious liberty.

Religion, after all—at least in the shadow of Protestantism—is something intensely personal and interior, something that law has only limited capacity to regulate and restrain, however hard it tries. When people are motivated by loyalty to something higher and greater than the state, they will defy the government's every effort to force them into conformity. The polities of early modern Europe quickly discovered this, as religious differences multiplied in the wake of the Reformation and Protestant rulers refused to continue the inquisitional techniques the medieval church had employed to suppress dissent. Many thinkers and statesmen, while still believing that public religious uniformity was, in theory, best for both individuals and society as a whole, began to recognize that they must make concessions to the facts on the ground. Individuals must be given the right to choose their own religious communities and practices.

One landmark in this development was England's 1689 Act of Toleration, which granted extensive civil liberties to nonconforming Protestants. The act found its most persuasive proponent and defender in philosopher John Locke, whose *Letter Concerning Toleration* (1689), together with his *Second Treatise on Civil Government* (1690), secured his reputation as the "father of liberalism." Today, Locke is caught in a tug-of-war between "liberals" and "postliberals"—celebrated by some for helping usher in the era of individual liberty that Americans take for granted every time we surf the internet without censorship and lamented by others for creating the conditions for a culture of licentiousness, shorn of tradition and emptied of public virtue. Locke's own aims were certainly more modest than the legacy we attribute to him today. True, he did seek to restrict the task of government to the protection of life and property—a far cry from the more comprehensive ambitions of the classical politics of ancient Greece or the Renaissance. But Locke believed strongly in the objectivity of natural law and public virtue, and he even recognized—unlike Jefferson a century later—that theological beliefs could be matters of grave political concern. Atheists and Catholics, for instance, were beyond the bounds of the toleration he advocated, since neither could be counted on to keep oaths or vows.[11]

Perhaps most significantly, Locke's emphasis on the language of "toleration" clearly sets him apart from liberalism as we have come to know it in the past few decades. While recognizing that well-educated citizens would form sometimes widely different visions of how best to conduct their lives and that it would be counterproductive to try to force them all into one common mold, Locke hardly celebrated this as a positive good. Among the early fathers of liberalism, including the American Founders, you will never find such slogans as "diversity is our strength" or "let a thousand flowers bloom." To call for tolerating something is at the same time to acknowledge it as an objective evil—something we wish did not exist but which it is useless to try to abolish. To speak this way nowadays would be seen as the height of intolerance. Consider the torrents of outrage provoked by actions as modest as a baker's polite refusal to make a cake for a same-sex wedding. This may neither pick the pockets nor break the legs of the gay or lesbian couple, but it will be perceived (and litigated) as an assault on their civic identity, a refusal to recognize them as equal members of society.

The sources of such a libertine conception of liberalism are many, of course, and technology has surely played at least as significant a role as ideas: in a society where most can afford to browse and choose between hundreds of different possible sofas, it will be hard not to think about freedom in very different

---

[11] According to official Roman Catholic teaching at that time, Catholics were permitted (and in some cases obliged) to violate any oaths made to heretics (including their Protestant rulers).

terms than in an era where you inherited the furniture your great-grandfather carved, and that was that. Still, if we were to point the finger at one thinker who helped change the way we think about liberty, it would be not John Locke but John Stuart Mill, whose 1864 essay "On Liberty" profoundly changed the terms of the discussion around political liberty.

Even for such advanced liberals as Thomas Jefferson, after all, there had been widespread agreement that (1) pursuing happiness meant pursuing virtue and (2) virtue was a real, objective, singular thing, something that required a shared constellation of values and a shared set of social norms at the very least. Morality mattered. The great experiment of the Founding era was to see whether morality might be better secured and promoted by the informal pressure of social custom and good education, rather than by the hard hand of law. By most measures, the experiment was remarkably successful—at least for a time. In both England and America, the nineteenth century saw dramatic improvements in public morals and manners, even as laws were generally much less intrusive and more tolerant than in the past. Civil society mobilized itself in moral crusades that would have been unimaginable in previous centuries, such as the successful campaign to eradicate slavery and the partially successful campaign to reduce alcoholism.

John Stuart Mill, however, wasn't having it. Public morality was for him a straitjacket:

> Protection . . . against the tyranny of the magistrate is not enough: there needs protection against the tyranny of the prevailing opinion and feeling; against the tendency of society to impose, by other means than civil penalties, its own ideas and practices as rules of

conduct on those who dissent from them; to fetter the development, and, if possible, prevent the formation, of any individuality not in harmony with its ways, and compel all characters to fashion themselves upon the model of its own.[12]

From this new standpoint, diversity should be celebrated; the multiplication of subjective opinions and preferences is a positive good. Mill deplored a society of conformity and stifling public norms, the stuffy "Victorianism" we still malign today, and he wanted a world in which no one would be mocked or marginalized for being different. This—not the mere formal liberty under law that Locke had called for—was what freedom meant: "The only freedom which deserves the name, is that of pursuing our own good in our own way, so long as we do not attempt to deprive others of theirs, or impede their efforts to attain it. . . . Over himself, over his own body and mind, the individual is sovereign."[13]

Of course, Mill personally was rather less radical than his ideas might suggest. Aside from being a religious skeptic and an early proponent of women's rights, he was a fairly straitlaced Victorian gentleman. When he called for a radical new vision of society built around the promotion of individuality, he had little notion of what he was calling for, seemingly assuming that most of the polite manners and values that knit society together would carry on of their own accord, with just a little

---

[12] J. S. Mill, "On Liberty," in *On Liberty, Utilitarianism, and Other Essays*, ed. Mark Philp and Frederick Rosen (Oxford: Oxford University Press, 2015), 8.

[13] Mill, "On Liberty," 15.

loosening of the Victorian straitjacket to give well-mannered but eccentric freethinkers like himself a little more room to breathe. Indeed, Mill still believed in a certain kind of objective morality, complaining that too much conformity interfered with real moral progress. It would be left to others, such as the playwright Oscar Wilde in the next generation, to push the envelope further, shocking contemporary sensibilities by an open display of the kind of transgressive individuality (in the form of sexual libertinism) implied by Mill's theory of liberty.

A century downstream from Mill and Wilde, we find that a liberalism of tolerating difference has quickly morphed into a liberalism of celebrating difference. The task of politics, in turn, has evolved from one of merely protecting individual rights to one of multiplying such rights. If freely chosen difference is a good thing, then the more choices and the more differences, the better. On this at least, the political "Left" and the political "Right" have been united for at least two generations. For decades, political conservatives lionized the economic philosophy of Milton Friedman (put into political practice by Ronald Reagan), which Friedman summarized in his 1980 bestseller *Free to Choose: A Personal Statement*. The glory of the market economy, on this account, was its continual expansion of the opportunities for consumer choice, thereby making possible more and more individuality and, it was to be presumed, more and more happiness. Meanwhile, those on the political Left may have deplored the excesses of unrestrained capitalism but found their own outlet for self-expression in the sexual revolution—which, nearly six decades on, has not yet run its course but continues to seek new frontiers of human nature to transgress, new bulwarks of civilizational order to demolish. For decades now, our two main political parties have been locked in a joint conspiracy to expand "freedom" and multiply "rights," with scarce a thought given to securing the moral, cultural, and political conditions within which these terms can have any meaning or durability. The result, of course, is a deepening bondage to individual whim and desire, a sense of futility or paralysis that comes from the loss of any shared sense of purpose, and a war of all against all as each individual seeks to assert his or her rights against one another.

The Liberty of Law

A Christian vision of political freedom, then, can never be satisfied with such liberty as mere maximization of individual "rights"; in a sinful world, we cannot accept the maxim that "that government is best which governs least," and we cannot equate happiness with the maximal space for the maximization of personal choice. Does this mean, however, turning back the clock to the life of the Greek polis or embracing a totalitarian moralism in which government forces us to discover "true freedom" through obedience?

Thankfully not. For there exists at least a third tradition of thinking about political liberty that has ancient roots and dominated the understanding of the American Founders. We may call it, for shorthand, "freedom as self-government," with the word "self" gesturing in both communal and individual directions.

Within this vision of freedom, a community or society is free inasmuch as it has the power to govern itself; but it is free only insofar as it actually governs itself—that is, inasmuch as it exercises its liberty through the purposeful ordering of law.

The liberty thus experienced is a collective liberty, reflecting our instinctive tendency to extend our sense of selfhood outward into family, tribe, and nation. Thus it was that in the time of the American Revolution, Americans protested not against the fact that they were being taxed but that *they were not taxing themselves*. To be sure, most people don't like being taxed at all; and after winning independence, many early Americans grumbled against their new governments as well. But in principle at least, they objected to British policy not so much because it violated their individual liberties but because it violated their corporate liberties. Acting through their state legislatures or local assemblies, early Americans had no problem passing laws that reflected and enforced their ideals of public virtue.[14]

The great threat to liberty in this older understanding was not authority per se, as it is for restless modern individualists, but arbitrary authority, authority unbound by law. The Founding era is full of denunciations of the "arbitrary." Consider one of the classic early statements of the colonists' cause, James Otis's *The Rights of the British Colonies Asserted and Proved* (1763). In it, he enumerates six fundamental rights for which the colonists contend, all of which in some way revolve around this concept, but two of which name it specifically:

> 3dly. No legislative, supreme or subordinate, has a right to make itself arbitrary.
>
> 4thly. The supreme legislative cannot justly assume a power of ruling by extempore arbitrary decrees, but is

---

[14] See for instance Barry Alan Shain's excellent study, *The Myth of American Individualism: The Protestant Origins of American Political Thought* (Princeton: Princeton University Press, 1994).

bound to dispense justice by known settled rules, and by duly authorized independant [sic] judges.[15]

An arbitrary power is a power of mere will. It is, as it were, mere power or absolute power in the most precise sense of the term: power unconstrained and unbound. In Christian theology, even God himself does not exercise power of this sort; rather, his power is limited by his own "eternal law," a model of perfect reason. Inspired by this theological analogy, early modern political thinkers, including the American Founders, insisted that true political authority was not found in arbitrary power but in power limited by the rule of law, "a government of laws rather than men," as John Adams declared in his attack on the arbitrary power of Parliament.[16]

This, then, was the first point to be made about freedom from arbitrary power: it was the freedom to be governed and to live "by known settled rules," whether these took the shape of immemorial customs or formally promulgated laws. Indeed, when one reads the Declaration of Independence, one is struck to find that its most recurrent complaint is that Britain had interfered with the colonists' ability to pass laws.

Government by Consent

At this point, we should be struck by the congruence between this idea of political freedom and what we learned in the past

---

[15] James Otis, *The Rights of the British Colonies Asserted and Proved* (1763), in *The American Republic: Primary Sources*, ed. Bruce Frohnen (Indianapolis: Liberty Fund, 2002), 121.

[16] John Adams, *Novanglus* (1774–75), in *The Political Writings of John Adams*, ed. George W. Carey (Washington, DC: Regnery, 2000), 66.

two chapters. *Spiritual freedom*, we observed, emerges when God liberates the individual from forgetfulness, futility, and fear: from the loss of agency that comes in being disconnected from our past, from the loss of agency that comes from uncertainty about what lies ahead, and from the loss of agency that comes from our inability to pursue any fixed purposes in the present. This last futility is closely associated, as we saw in chapter 3, with the lack of *moral freedom*, as we find ourselves pulled to and fro by irrational passions and warring desires. The same things are true of a political society that lacks the rule of law—or that is governed by laws it has no ability to shape and understand.

Citizens in such a society will be forced to live from moment to moment, cut off from their past because they are unsure of what will be the next set of norms handed down from on high. They will be crippled by fear and uncertainty, wondering whether deeds that are laudable today might not be prosecutable tomorrow. And they will see little point in undertaking any great collective activities because they will not know whether the conditions that made those activities seem great and worthwhile yesterday will continue. It is no exaggeration to call such a condition a form of slavery. Such a feeling of slavery might be avoided by living under a rule of law so perfect, so rational, and so benevolent that everyone could be confident that it would always serve their flourishing—but that ideal is unattainable on this sinful earth. If we must live under fallible or imperfect laws, then, the only way to secure political freedom is to live under laws that, at least in some sense, reflect our own consent, laws by which we govern ourselves.

However, we must pause to consider what "consent" does and doesn't mean. We hear a lot about consent these days—indeed, it has become almost the sole remaining basis for restraining sexual self-indulgence—but it has subtly shifted its meaning, as its use in sex education highlights. Consent, we are told, is something that can be given or withheld on any basis whatsoever, and from moment to moment. Consent can be withdrawn at any time, and anyone's decision to do so must be absolutely respected. This may be a good standard to use in sexual intercourse (though it should hardly be the only standard), but it is obviously a terrible standard to use for consent in political society. Applied in this way, the idea that authority rests on the "consent of the governed" represents an effective abandonment of authority altogether. If nothing can be done as soon as anyone objects for any reason, then that will mean the end of all lawmaking and law enforcement. Indeed, we will find ourselves back in the domain not of liberty but of tyranny, enslaved not to one arbitrary will but to millions of arbitrary wills.

What then did our ancestors mean by the word "consent"? For them, consent was embodied in time-tested customs and communal practices, unwritten laws that written laws should respect. Consent was also exercised above all in the solemn business of making vows and promises. Indeed, that is what voting and lawmaking were all about: these were great corporate acts of promise-making, by which individuals covenanted before God to bind themselves to the actions of their representatives, and the representatives in turn covenanted before God to bind themselves (and those they represented) to follow the laws they enacted. Such laws could of course be revised or rescinded, but this required just as much solemnity and seriousness as lawmaking; and in the meantime, the laws must stand. Only by this means could a political community have the freedom to act reliably and purposefully in pursuit of its common good—and in that good, promote the flourishing of each of its members.

From this standpoint, we can readily see why the American Founders were so fond of saying things like, "Our constitution was designed for a moral and religious people. It is wholly inadequate to the government of any other."[17] Self-government, in the corporate sense, rested upon the foundation of self-government in an individual sense: on individuals attentive to the voice of conscience and armed against the storms of passion. Only citizens who were each capable of holding steadfast to their commitments and promises would be collectively capable of making and submitting to laws. Otherwise, allowing their passions to run riot, they would either pass laws to oppress one another or, disdaining the authority of law altogether, generate anarchy that only a strongman or dictator would be able to overcome. "Will men never be free?" exclaimed Samuel Adams. "They will be free no longer than while they remain virtuous."[18] Republican self-government could only be limited government as long as there remained a basic foundation of individual self-government. If individuals were largely governing themselves, keeping both their tempers and their promises, they did not need draconian laws or ubiquitous surveillance and policing to maintain peace and order. If, however, moral self-government began to unravel, violence would increase, cheating would become more common, and trust would begin to crumble throughout

---

[17] John Adams, "Letter to the Massachusetts Militia" (October 11, 1798), at *Founders Online*, https://founders.archives.gov/documents/Adams/99-02-02-3102.

[18] Quoted in Thomas Kidd, *God of Liberty: A Religious History of the American Revolution* (New York: Basic Books, 2012), 98.

society. Every contract would have to be enforced by the courts, and peaceful neighborhoods would depend on pervasive police forces. And the bigger government got, the less it could actually be responsive to the people. As Daniel Dreisbach summarizes the Founding era consensus: "A self-governing people, in short, had to be a virtuous people who were controlled from within by an internal moral compass."[19]

Political freedom, then, rests on a foundation of moral freedom. But what about spiritual freedom? Does this vision of liberty as republican self-government depend in any way on what we have learned about the spiritual freedom of a Christian before God? Well, yes—and not just because moral freedom, as we have seen, is only fully attainable from within the context of the spiritual freedom offered by the gospel of grace.

Durable political freedom requires a context in which citizens do not live in fear of the authority of government but do not despise this authority either. They must simultaneously respect it and be able to laugh at it, and both for the same reason—because it is ordained by God, existing only under and through his authorization. So, Paul teaches in Romans 13 and Peter in 1 Peter 2. The magistrate "does not bear the sword in vain" (Rom 13:4) and acts as an instrument of God's wrath—a fearful prospect. And yet we are to "have no fear of the one who is in authority" if we can simply "do what is good" by walking in love (v. 3; cf. vv. 8–10). An ungodly ruler, as the example of many a biblical saint shows, can be cheerfully disregarded if he commands us to act against God, because the believer's conscience is captive to the Word of God. Outside such cases, the ungodly

---

[19] Daniel L. Dreisbach, *Reading the Bible with the Founding Fathers* (Oxford: Oxford University Press, 2017), 68.

ruler can also be cheerfully tolerated, however inconvenient, as David showed in his continued loyalty to a corrupt King Saul. From the standpoint of the liberated Christian conscience, government just isn't something to get that worked up about.

But only a conscience truly at peace before God can enjoy such political tranquility. For if we are not sure that God is well-pleased with us, as both Augustine and Luther observed, we will seek ephemeral rest in trying to win favor from our fellow men. Whether it be the slavish flattery of those in authority or the smug satisfaction that comes from being part of a band of rowdy revolutionaries, we will seek our salvation in politics, one way or another. And if there is one consistent message of Scripture, it is that all idolatry leads to slavery.

Spiritual freedom, moral freedom, political freedom. These three, as we have seen, name very different ideals, yet all three are longed-for objects of human striving. All three, however, are knit together: spiritual freedom makes possible both moral and political freedom; moral freedom both fosters and is fostered by political freedom; political freedom, in the proper sense, helps nurture a society in which the gospel has room to do its work, a society of truly free men and women. With this map of the landscape now clear before us, I will turn in the last three chapters to look at three major battlegrounds of freedom in the world today: technology, economy, and religious exercise.

5

Freedom and Technology: The Faustian Bargain of Modern Life

> Then they said, "Come, let us build ourselves
> a city and a tower with its top in the heavens,
> and let us make a name for ourselves, lest we be
> dispersed over the face of the whole earth."
> —Genesis 11:4

> The difference between technology and slavery is
> that slaves are fully aware that they are not free.
> —Nassim Nicholas Taleb, *The Bed of Procrustes*

"You Will Be Like God"

Mankind was made for freedom—but what kind of freedom? Not a freedom to do just anything but a freedom to rule as kings, to take dominion over creation as image bearers of the great

King. This was a freedom bound by the limits of creaturehood, but a freedom enjoyed at the very highest reaches of creaturehood and intended for even greater exaltation and glory, if Adam and Eve had passed the test. But they just didn't have the patience. "Take and eat, and you will be like God," the serpent promised. Kingship and queenship were not enough; Adam and Eve longed for the freedom of infinitude. And strangely enough, they believed that creation itself—a fruit grown from the dust of the earth—could give them the power that belonged only to the Creator.

This is the temptation that technology poses in every age: the lure of transcending our limits, becoming gods, and doing so *without the trouble of waiting*. Technology promises us reward without labor—or at any rate, more reward with less labor. With technology, we take the stuff of creation, which we have been called to guard and keep, and use it to rival and defy our Creator. Just in case we didn't get the message from Genesis 3, God repeats it in a second fall narrative in Genesis 11. This time, it is not a fruit grown from the dust of the ground that will enable man to reach the heavens but bricks baked from the dust of the ground. With their extraordinary technological abilities, men were able to build "a city and a tower with its top in the heavens" and thus to "make a name [for themselves]" (Gen 11:4), rather than waiting in patient devotion upon the name that is above every name. Recognizing the power of human ingenuity, God discerns the peril that awaits our effort to transcend the limits of our creatureliness: "This is only the beginning of what they will do. And nothing that they propose to do will now be impossible for them" (Gen 11:6). Sure enough, it was only the beginning of what we would do. Today we have pierced the heavens and walked on the moon; we have split the atom and called down fire from heaven upon our enemies.

But of course, technology is not all bad—far from it. We were made, after all, to take dominion over the creatures, to transform the voiceless creation that it might give voice to the glory of God through art and music and metalworking. Genesis testifies to the deep ambiguity of all our technology by attributing the earliest technologies—music-making and metallurgy—to the descendants of Cain (see Gen 4:21–22). If we are tempted to view such works as evil in themselves, Scripture quickly rebukes us in Exodus, where these Cainite technologies become the instruments of the Spirit for the glory of God: "See, I have called by name Bezalel the son of Uri, son of Hur, of the tribe of Judah, and I have filled him with the Spirit of God, with ability and intelligence, with knowledge and all craftsmanship, to devise artistic designs, to work in gold, silver, and bronze, in cutting stones for setting, and in carving wood, to work in every craft" (Exod 31:2–5). When David reforms the tabernacle worship and Solomon builds the temple, the technologies of music-making are likewise offered in service to the Creator. And when in Revelation 21, the kings of the earth bring their glory into the New Jerusalem, we can be confident that this glory includes the astonishing fruits of human technology over the millennia.

Technology is not merely a means by which we bring the original hidden glories of creation to full expression. It is also a means by which we resist, and in some measure roll back, the curse of Genesis 3. If we turn to technology to reduce human labor, who can blame us, in a world where creation itself now fights against us and increases all our labors? "Cursed is the ground because of you. . . . By the sweat of your face you shall eat bread" (Gen 3:17, 19)—but rather less sweat, thankfully, in the age of the tractor and the combine. "I will surely multiply your pain in childbearing; in pain you shall bring forth children" (Gen 3:16)—but rather less pain, we may be grateful, in the age of modern medicine. Indeed, even the most determined Luddite among us, I feel sure, does not want to go back to a world before antiseptics and anesthetics, a world in which a large share of pregnancies ended in agonizing deaths for both mother and child.

What is technology, then? A God-given tool for mitigating the pain of the curse? A manifestation of our original calling to take dominion over the world? Or a means by which we try to turn creation itself against the Creator, straining against the limits of our finitude so that we might be as gods? Clearly, it can be all three. It can be a means of resisting the bondage of sin and death, of expressing our original creative freedom, and of ultimately destroying our freedom in a search for a freedom that is not ours to enjoy. To use technology for true freedom requires a wisdom and a discernment beyond our years, especially as new technologies emerge faster than we can wrap our heads around them. But we have no choice except to do our best to grow into such wisdom.

The Irishman's Two Stoves

Although technology has always been with us, it is hard to resist the sense that something has changed profoundly in the past century or two. Once we were the masters, and technology our servant; today we feel increasingly at the mercy of our own creations. Once we *developed* particular technologies, instruments to perform given tasks; now we seem simply to *inhabit* a world of technology. This technological world seems to be an all-encompassing reality from which it is difficult to escape and difficult to lay hold of any piece of creation that we have not already reordered in our image. Even if we have the good fortune to behold an unspoiled mountain vista or sublime waterfall, we are likely to admire it only through the lens of our smartphone, reducing the world to digital form so we can use it to build up our online followings. With the emergence of new digital and biotechnologies, we are at greater and greater risk of trying to make ourselves gods and, in the process, rendering ourselves slaves.

What has shifted? Well, according to C. S. Lewis, diagnosing the change underway eight decades ago in his *Abolition of Man*, the object of our technologies has shifted. Once we worked primarily on the raw material of the lower creation, on rocks and dirt, plants, and occasionally animals. Now we work upon human nature itself, both our bodies (in the form of biotechnology) and our minds (in the form of digital technology). Initially, we turned our technologies upon ourselves with an eye to healing the hurts of the curse of Genesis—diseases, tumors, and broken bones—thus seeking to restore our bodies to their proper natural operation. Increasingly, though, we are using the same technologies to try to free ourselves from the very limits of creaturehood, to achieve an abolition of the slavery of simply being human. This, as Lewis observed, was a fool's errand, for our progressive quest to free ourselves from the constraints of nature must backfire once it passes this point: "It is like the famous Irishman who found that a certain kind of stove reduced his fuel bill by half and thence concluded that two stoves of the same kind would enable him to warm his house with no fuel at all."[1] Once we turn our technologies upon ourselves with the idea of remaking the human condition, we are both the subject and the object of this power, master and slave: "Each new power won by man is a power over man as well. Each advance leaves him weaker as well as stronger. In every victory, besides being the general who triumphs, he is also the prisoner who follows the triumphal car."[2]

"Nothing" Is Very Strong

Nowhere are the godlike pretensions of modern technology more apparent than in the digital realm; nowhere else do the warnings of Genesis 3 echo so loudly. With the digital world, it seems, we have finally found a way to escape the basic limitations of creatureliness, the constraints of time and space, the stubborn resistance of materiality. We can, like the characters in the profound technology parable *Inception*, "make our own world" by generating images and experiences that would be impossible in the real world, living out fantasy lives that provide escape from the dreariness of the ones God has called us to. We can also aspire to godlike knowledge, with nearly instantaneous access to nearly everything that has ever been known. We can do all this with the absolute minimum of effort. Eve at least had to reach up and pick a fruit to "be like God." All we have to do is swipe a forefinger.

Nowhere else do we see so clearly the self-defeating, self-enslaving character of the modern quest for technological

---

[1] C. S. Lewis, *The Abolition of Man* (New York: Macmillan, 1960), 45.
[2] Lewis, 37.

liberation. In one of the most memorable of *The Screwtape Letters*, Lewis describes the condition of man in the grip of *acedia*, the world-weariness that drags us away from God and into the Nothing:

> You can make him waste his time not only in conversation he enjoys with people whom he likes, but in conversations with those he cares nothing about on subjects that bore him. You can make him do nothing at all for long periods. You can keep him up late at night, not roistering, but staring at a dead fire in a cold room. All the healthy and out-going activities which we want him to avoid can be inhibited and *nothing* given in return, so that at least he may say, as one of my own patients said on his arrival down here, "I now see that I spent most of my life in doing *neither* what I ought *nor* what I liked." . . . Nothing is very strong: strong enough to steal away a man's best years not in sweet sins but in a dreary flickering of the mind over it knows not what and knows not why, in the gratification of curiosities so feeble that the man is only half aware of them, in drumming of fingers and kicking of heels, in whistling tunes that he does not like, or in the long, dim labyrinth of reveries that have not even lust or ambition to give them a relish, but which once chance association has started them, the creature is too weak and fuddled to shake off.[3]

Such a state of self-alienation is nothing new to the digital age. Lewis says that "a column of advertisements in yesterday's

---

[3] C. S. Lewis, *The Screwtape Letters* (New York: HarperCollins, 2001), 59–60.

paper will do."[4] But it has never been easier than in the age of the smartphone, when anything or nothing is sufficient to attract our wandering attention to the glowing, vibrating screen in our pocket. A family of five sits silently on a train, oblivious to the breathtaking scenery outside—not because they are absorbed in conversation with one another but because each alone is absorbed in his or her phone. A teenager stays up late at night, not celebrating with friends but staring at images on a screen in a cold dark room. You tire momentarily of the conversation at a party, and rather than expending an ounce of effort to enliven it with a witty observation, you pull out your phone and scroll idly through the latest posts by people you care nothing about on subjects that bore you. The holidays pass, and you realize you have wasted them not in rest or recreation but in the gratification of digital curiosities so feeble that you are only half aware of them but which you are too weak and fuddled to shake off.

The darkest, cruelest, and most enslaving form of this phenomenon is of course pornography, which sucks its users into dim labyrinths that have not even lust to give them a relish—only the lure of novelty, the promise of escape. But the soul-destroying power of internet pornography is really just a particularly vicious form of the soul-destroying power of the internet generally, with its endless parade of images and information stoking an unquenchable thirst for novelty, a restless, aimless foraging that seems to leave us hungrier and emptier the more media we consume.[5] Just as pornography renders its users

---

[4] Lewis, 59.

[5] For some particularly insightful remarks on this theme, see Samuel D. James, *Digital Liturgies: Rediscovering Christian Wisdom in an Online Age* (Wheaton, IL: Crossway, 2023), chap. 7.

less able to experience or enjoy real sexual partnership, so do all our bad habits of digital addiction distract us from all "healthy and outgoing activities" and give nothing in return.[6] The more time we spend looking at perfect sunsets on Instagram and trying to capture our own, the less we are able to appreciate a sunset. The more effort we expend trying to curate the perfect image of our family life for social media, the less we will be able to enjoy our children, messiness and all. The more we engage in 280-character shouting matches, the less we will be able to carry on and profit from an actual debate of perspectives. The more we resort to the gif- and emoji-laden snippets of chat threads, the less likely we will be to ever know the surpassing joys and uproarious laughter of a real conversation.

In each case, digital technology promises us the freedom of boundlessness, liberated from the constraints of time and space that govern everyday life, freed from the friction that comes with any physical interaction. And in each case, we find that we have simply forged new chains for ourselves: unable to discipline our own impulses to swipe and click, unable to maintain boundaries around our own time and sanity, unable to remember after thirty minutes of web-browsing what we were even looking for and why, we learn again the hard way that freedom is actually *constituted* by limits, limits that technology relentlessly devours.

Who's to Blame?

In *The Abolition of Man*, Lewis also warns us not to delude ourselves with the popular idea that technology is wielded equally by

---

[6] Lewis, *The Screwtape Letters*, 59.

all. The socialist utopia of equally shared ownership of the means of production is a pipe dream. "What we call Man's power over Nature turns out to be a power exercised by some men over other men with Nature as its instrument,"[7] Lewis warns. He immediately stresses that this does not mean that people will necessarily abuse such power—they may use it with the most benevolent of intentions. But the fact remains that this is simply what technology *means* in a world of unequal distribution of resources: the acquisition of new tools by certain people, corporations, or nations that will confer power over other people, corporations, or nations. Nowhere, perhaps, is this truer than in the realm of digital technology. Although the internet emerged over three decades ago with the promise of liberation and democratization, giving every human being equal access to a world of information and creative potential, today it is dominated by a handful of gigantic firms with greater global market power than any firms in history.[8]

Faced with this power imbalance and our deepening dissatisfaction over our digital predicament, it is tempting to turn and bite the hand that has fed us for the past couple of decades. Acclaimed books like Shoshana Zuboff's *Age of Surveillance Capitalism* have exposed the perverse incentives at the heart of much of the Big Tech business model: creating ever-more-addictive products to ensure ever-more "engaged" users, so as to extract more and more behavioral data to sell to advertisers.[9]

---

[7] Lewis, *Abolition of Man*, 35.

[8] See Josh Hawley, *The Tyranny of Big Tech* (Washington, DC: Regnery, 2021).

[9] Shoshana Zuboff, *The Age of Surveillance Capitalism: The Fight for a Human Future at the New Frontier of Power* (New York: PublicAffairs, 2019).

While subsequent legislative reforms and user revolts have modified the picture somewhat, there is no sense pretending that most digital technology represents a happy, healthy "free market" in which firms are simply supplying customers with the products and services that will improve their quality of life.[10] Still, we should not pretend either that all of us are simply passive victims of tyrannical Big Tech titans. Many of us have been willing accomplices of our own enslavement. Consider the frequent bursts of outrage about consumer "privacy" in the face of all-pervasive digital surveillance.

There are good reasons to seek privacy, of course, but often our search for privacy is motivated by shame. No sooner did Adam and Eve commit the first sin than they tried to enter "incognito mode," hiding their nakedness with fig leaves and cowering in the bushes to avoid divine accountability. From that day to this, human beings have longed for a way to keep their sins to themselves. But this is rendered difficult by our need for community. Given the weakness and fragility of our natures, we, unlike many animals, have to live in close contact with others of our kind, and these human communities tend to keep an eye on the behavior of its members. With the rise of the internet, it became conceivable for the first time in history to enjoy many of the benefits of life in society without the burden of such accountability. Far more than any previous generation, we have found a way to escape from the prying eyes of neighbors and authorities and pursue our private pastimes or vices without leaving any trace on the social world around us. Indeed, if we ever forget to enter "incognito mode," we can with a single click

---

[10] This misleading idea of the "free market" is a theme we will explore more fully in the next chapter.

of a button do what every sinner has longed to do since Eden: *delete history*.

The reality is that most of us are quite happy to accept the ubiquitous surveillance of Big Data as a substitute for the intrusive personal accountability of yesteryear. We no longer watch over one another, those closest to us; and grateful for this liberation, we are happy to let Meta and Google watch over us instead. If we can escape being manipulated by our parents, pastors, and spouses, we reason, we are more than willing to let ourselves be manipulated by targeted advertisers and feed aggregators.

Lewis wrote *The Abolition of Man* at the high-water mark of "rational scientific planning," in the midst of a world war in which two great powers (Germany and Russia) represented different forms of the cult of scientific management applied on a national scale, and in which even the free nations were forced to resort to massive central planning to meet the demands of total war. Many in the West hoped that out of the war would emerge a utopian era of a peaceful and orderly society, ensured by rational scientists conditioning human nature and guiding it toward some higher stage of evolution; but Lewis knew too much about human psychology to believe in such dreams. The reality, he discerned, was that most of these posthuman schemers would be animated chiefly by the same animal desires (for money, sex, and power) that had stimulated most of the powerful men throughout the ages, and all the more so now that they had rejected traditional conceptions of human nature and morality.[11] However, perhaps Lewis still gave too much credence to

---

[11] "It is not that they are bad men. They are not men at all. Stepping outside the *Tao*, they have stepped into the void. . . . All

the myth of scientific management—the idea that the future direction of society would be determined by a handful of men in lab coats and their political enablers lurking underneath. The reality is that, by and large, our technocratic elites—whether in Silicon Valley or Washington, DC—are simply giving us what we demand, feeding the ravenous appetites of a humanity whose god is its belly.

Having promised ourselves a brave new world in which humankind could be freed from natural limitations to pursue some higher purpose, a new order of the ages in which justice and equality at last would reign, we find ourselves staggering drunkenly after each fresh technological innovation for nothing more than the mere pleasure it promises. Or, to come nearer to the depressing truth, we grasp frantically after each new technology as a drug to dull the pain of a world from which every real pleasure has been banished, as a distraction to keep at bay the Nothingness into which we feel ourselves spiraling after we have traded away our very humanity in pursuit of cheap thrills.

Selling Our Souls to Be Free from Our Bodies

If this is true of the digital revolution, it is perhaps even more true of the revolution in biotechnology that has equally conspired to change our conception over the past half a century of

---

motives that claim any validity other than that of their felt emotional weight at a given moment have failed them. Everything except the *sic volo, sic jubeo* ["as I wish, thus I command"] has been explained away. . . . The Conditioners, therefore, must come to be motivated simply by their own pleasure." Lewis, *Abolition of Man*, 65.

what it means to be human. For all the great life-saving developments in medical technology of the past half-century, our era will no doubt be remembered by history for a string of new medical techniques and social practices all centered on that strongest of all animal desires: sex. "If man chooses to treat himself as raw material," writes Lewis, "raw material he will be: not raw material to be manipulated, as he fondly imagined, by himself, but by mere appetite, mere Nature."[12]

Although we may increasingly live our lives and pursue our pleasures in the digital realm, we still find ourselves stubbornly inhabiting physical bodies, and it is over these physical bodies that the greatest cultural and theological battles of our time are still fought. When Lewis penned his prescient warnings of the technological perils before us in *The Abolition of Man* and *That Hideous Strength*, he had in mind chiefly the advances of medical and genetic techniques that threatened to conquer human nature itself. Eight decades on, those prophecies have largely come true through the practices of abortion on demand, artificial insemination and *in vitro* fertilization, genetic manipulation of embryos, and most visibly and jarringly, the transgender revolution. Through all these practices and more, we Westerners have manifested our grotesquely misguided idea of freedom as the transcendence of all limits, up to and including the limits off our bodily nature itself.

The result has been a fundamental transformation in the concept and practice of medicine, which was once committed to the maxim "first, do no harm." By this principle, physicians demonstrated their recognition that the capabilities of

---

[12] Lewis, 45.

medical technique were bound to the norms of bodily health, a good that the tools of the physician could as readily imperil as enhance. Our word *health* comes from the same root as our word *whole*. To restore something to health, it used to be understood, meant to bring it back to its fullness. The art of healthcare was, quite simply, aimed at the good of the body, conceived in terms of its proper functioning. Disease or injury impeded the body from attaining its natural goodness, and it was the task of medicine to restore it. There were, of course, any number of things that medicine *could* do, as a matter of pure technique—lop off a limb at random or cause a patient's lungs to fill with fluid—but to do these would no longer be *medicine*, whose first rule is "do no harm." The current craze for "transgender healthcare," then, is a contradiction in terms, at least as usually practiced.

According to the policies of an increasing number of developed countries, the use of a mastectomy to treat breast cancer is to be deemed medically indistinguishable from a mastectomy to turn a thirteen-year-old girl into a "boy."[13] Any procedure formerly devised to treat some particular physical disease or condition now needs to be on the table to treat a wholly different—and purely psychological—condition. This represents the complete divorce of medicine from *healthcare*, understood as the restoration of a body to its proper good. Instead, we have the new idea

---

[13] See, for instance, Rachel N. Morrison, "HHS Proposed Non-discrimination Regulations Impose Transgender Mandate in Health Care," *FedSoc Blog*, September 8, 2022, https://fedsoc.org/commentary/fedsoc-blog/hhs-s-proposed-nondiscrimination-regulations-impose-transgender-mandate-in-health-care-1.

of medicine as pure technological power to achieve whatever results the patient—or his manipulative clinicians—desire.

This transformation is the result of the substitution of *freedom* for health as the ultimate end of healthcare. Under the new conception, palsy is bad not because it impairs the natural functioning of a patient's nervous system and muscles but because it limits her freedom. By the same token, then, an unwanted pregnancy or even an unwanted set of sexual organs demands medical intervention just as surely, and for the same reasons, as a diagnosis of palsy or appendicitis. As Oliver O'Donovan wrote in his 1984 *Begotten or Made*:

> Technology derives its social significance from the fact that by it man has discovered new freedoms from necessity. The technological transformation of the modern age has gone hand in hand with the social and political quest of Western man to free himself from the necessities imposed upon him by religion, society, and nature. . . . Medical technique, too, has been shaped and developed with the intention of fulfilling aspirations for freedom, freedom in this case from the necessities imposed upon us by our bodily nature.[14]

Once human nature itself is treated as an enemy to be conquered, however, the boundary between self-transcendence and self-destruction, between freedom and slavery, becomes indistinguishable. "Once our souls, that is, our selves, have been given up," writes Lewis, "the power thus conferred will

---

[14] Oliver O'Donovan, *Begotten or Made?: A New Edition for the 21st Century* (Landrum, SC: Davenant, 2022), 7.

not belong to us. We shall in fact be the slaves and puppets of that to which we have given our souls."[15]

Breaking the Shackles

If our quest for godlike freedom finds its terminus in such bondage, how should we as Christians respond? Is there any escape from the dystopian trajectory of our technological age?

Well, we should begin at least by resisting such dystopian thoughts. I have deliberately emphasized the darker side of modern technologies, but there are plenty of other stories to be told as well—of organ transplants and prosthetic limbs, of the digitization of countless libraries of knowledge, of telescopes that can discern the fingerprints of God in the farthest recesses of space. The first step toward restoring a healthy posture toward our technologies is to start asking the most basic questions of them: What are they for? What are we doing with them? What are they doing to us? We must remember the cardinal truth that just because we *can* do something doesn't mean we *should*. Too often, drunk on the heady fumes of scientific progress, we have allowed ourselves to push the limits of what our ingenuity can achieve and then to assume that now that we've broken through some former barrier, it's time to bring the new gadget to market or put the new algorithm to work. But why? Just because we have been clever enough to discover or produce new poisons doesn't mean we drink them. One of the greatest of all scientific breakthroughs—the atomic bomb—is an invention that humanity has wisely refrained from using ever since.

---

[15] Lewis, *Abolition of Man*, 45.

We must be prepared to exercise such discernment and self-restraint—individual and collective—when it comes to many of the most fashionable technologies, from *in vitro* fertilization to TikTok. This will mean different things to different people depending on our vocations. For individuals, it will mean cultivating anew the virtue of patience. This might mean not just waiting a bit longer for something but, in some cases, waiting until the resurrection. Human life means accepting limits and accepting suffering; when technology offers us an apparent escape route, we should examine it closely to see if it is not in fact merely a shimmering mirage. Infertility, for instance, is a great suffering for many couples, but accustoming ourselves to the manufacture of embryos is a greater evil. Loneliness and boredom are perhaps a milder but more ubiquitous suffering, but we should resist the siren song of social media, which will not provide the true balm our restless hearts desire. For Christians involved in designing, producing, and marketing new technologies, humility and charity are in order: Have I really come up with a brilliant new invention or just a quick way to make more money? Will this new product or procedure *actually benefit* my customers or patients? If not, there's nothing wrong with sticking with the status quo, at the risk of being called old-fashioned.

Of course, we do not just live in a world with technologies but in a technological world. We are not mere individual consumers deciding which phone to buy, but we find ourselves embedded in social structures that increasingly take the newest technologies for granted. In 2003, no one had heard of a smartphone. By 2013, more than half of all new phones worldwide were smartphones. By 2023, it is becoming very difficult to function in modern society *without* a smartphone. In such a world, responsible individual choices will not be enough. Parents in particular have a critical responsibility to their children to help them grow into freedom, which means protecting them from premature exposure to the infinite spaces and godlike powers of the metaverse, until they have grown souls sturdy enough to resist its alluring promises and intense pressures. Civil authorities, whom the Christian tradition once referred to as "fathers of their people," should also step up to the plate and exercise paternal care, taking commonsense steps to restrict access to pornography and to quash medical malpractices like gender-reassignment surgery.

However, as technology is developing at an ever-greater pace, any specific prescriptions in this book will soon find themselves out of date. Even as I write, the AI revolution is bursting upon us, with consequences none can foretell. So I will resist the urge to say more about specific strategies for disciplining specific technologies here.

What does not change, however, is the human heart and the spiritual roots of our fascination with technology. Trapped in fear and guilt, we tend to hide our faces from God, who is the source of all good, and we thus lose our delight in all the goods he has given us. In this condition of spiritual unfreedom, we seek escape from the limits of embodiment, warring against nature or trying to distract ourselves from it among the evanescent vapors of our own creations. Or else we may travel in the other direction: even if we are in a state of relative spiritual health, we may begin to thoughtlessly habituate ourselves to the ecosystems of distraction that surround us until we begin to forget what it might feel like to truly *attend* to a poem or a person.

Our capacity for deep enjoyment thus destroyed, we quickly lose the capacity to enjoy the One who demands the most sustained attention of all. A lack of spiritual freedom may lead us to seek titillations that end in moral bondage; conversely, the careless sacrifice of our self-mastery may drive us inexorably into a state of spiritual unfreedom. Whichever direction we travel along this vicious circle, technology offers itself as a superhighway to speed our journey.

The way out of escape, then, requires effort in both directions. We must seek to reignite our love for God by worship, prayer, reading, and meditation, to be sure. And yet we will constantly find our minds clouded in the attempt if we are living slothful lives of perpetual distraction. We must ensure that whatever technologies we may need to make use of in our daily vocations, we are taking regular excursions back into the heart of creation, fixing our gaze on God's creatures rather than ours. It may sound naïve or clichéd to suggest that we can protect ourselves from the worst ravages of a technological age by taking a hike to admire a waterfall. But this is at least an important start. As we consciously cultivate a patient attention to the goods with which God has surrounded us, we will become less tempted to graze restlessly in search of the momentary diversions that technology promises. And the more capable we become of taking joy in the goods that come from God, the more we will be drawn in gratitude back to joyful fellowship with him, equipped with the spiritual and moral freedom to again take wise dominion over the world into which he has called us.

6

Freedom and the Market: Escaping the Bondage of Mammon

> For the love of money is a root of all kinds
> of evils. It is through this craving that some
> have wandered away from the faith and
> pierced themselves with many pangs.
> —1 Timothy 6:10

> They are as sick who surfeit with too much
> as they that starve with nothing.
> —Shakespeare, *The Merchant of Venice*

> You have made us for yourself, O Lord, and our
> hearts are restless until they rest in you.
> —Augustine, *Confessions*

What Is a Free Market?

When a modern American talks about freedom (especially if he or she is a politician), odds are he or she is talking in some way about economic freedom. For the generation after World War II, America's mission in the world was almost inseparable from its claim to represent "the free enterprise system" against the closed societies and command economies of the Soviet Union and its satellites. This point was sharpened by Milton Friedman and his disciples (among them Ronald Reagan) in the 1970s and 1980s, so that by the time the Berlin Wall fell in 1990, "free markets" eclipsed all else as the essential gift that the West sought to export to the rest of the world. Although American politics is ostensibly divided between a pro–free market Republican Party and a more ambivalent Democratic Party, almost everyone in American politics at least pays lip service to the ideal. But what is this ideal? What might it mean for a market to be free?

As we have seen repeatedly in these pages, a "freedom" that looks so simple on the surface turns out on closer inspection to be full of tensions or even contradictions. One person's freedom is quite liable to be another's unfreedom; a market that seeks to maximize the freedom of consumers may significantly constrain the freedom of producers, while a market geared to ensure the freedom of employers may feel like slavery for workers. And extreme freedom in any of these directions would undermine the freedom of all by destroying the conditions needed for a market to function.

Even if we consider only two of the key distinctions outlined in chapter 1, we will quickly see how divergent different visions of economic freedom may be. The proponent of a strictly *negative* liberty is liable to focus on the obstacles posed by laws and regulations to an individual's or business's freedom of action and will argue for a policy of libertarian nonintervention. Those concerned with *positive* liberty, however, may emphasize the material conditions of necessity imposed by poverty and may argue, as Franklin D. Roosevelt did, for "freedom from want" as a necessary condition of freedom, a condition that may require aggressive government intervention. Those concerned with *individual* liberty are liable to focus on the freedom of the consumer (since production, especially in modern economies, almost always requires large-scale cooperation) and will thus favor policies, like free trade, that maximize the number of options and minimize the prices facing consumers. Those concerned with *collective* liberty,[1] though, might be concerned about the freedom of the nation as a whole, which means promoting its economic independence from foreign supply chains that could weaken the nation or hold it hostage. Those people will accordingly *oppose* free trade. There is no easy answer to this latter debate, and indeed the two main parties have switched sides on it twice in the past century: originally, Democrats were avid free-traders while Republicans stressed its drawbacks, before the two parties swapped places in the latter half of the twentieth century. In just the past few years, Republicans have started to swing back toward protectionism in service of national freedom, while Democrats have embraced the idea of a borderless world in which individuals, goods, and services can go wherever they want.

---

[1] In earlier chapters I have called this "corporate liberty," but I substitute the term "collective" here to avoid confusion in this context.

As Christians, our instinctive temptation is to latch on to one or another of these rival visions of economic freedom and slap the label "biblical" or "Christlike" on it. There have been times and places where Christians have campaigned for socialism or even communism, a society in which every citizen is freed from poverty and the oppression of an employer, as the only authentically Christian economic system. Even today on the political left, it is not hard to find Christians framing their calls for redistribution as religious demands. Perhaps more common though, at least in America, has been the temptation to baptize free-market capitalism as God's own economic paradigm and to rummage through the Scriptures in search of proof-texts for the prescriptions of Milton Friedman and Friedrich Hayek. While there are certainly better and worse economic systems, true and false economic dogmas, we should always beware of making the Bible answer questions it was never written to address.

Indeed, such debates—in which the focus remains on the outward, bodily, political dimension of freedom—can readily distract us from the deeper forms of freedom and unfreedom that we have considered in this book. As we saw in the previous chapter about technology, it is entirely possible for our quest for ever-expanding outward freedom to go hand in hand with insidious forms of moral and spiritual bondage, such as the idolatrous habits of consumerism. Accordingly, in this chapter, while I will highlight some of the economic and political complexities involved in shaping a truly free market, it would be far too ambitious to offer policy solutions or delve into contested questions of economic theory. Some Christians are called to participate in such debates, but all of us, as I shall emphasize in closing, are called to reshaping our hearts away from the bondage of greed and toward the true freedom of resting in God.

The False Freedom of Consumerism

According to the idea of "a free market" most prevalent today among American Christians, the most important economic freedom is one that multiplies and maximizes our choices. A market free from regulation, so the story goes, is one in which free competition between producers will generate an ever-expanding range of products catering to every conceivable consumer taste, while also driving down prices so that the consumer can afford to choose between more and more items. Indeed, since the Industrial Revolution, such has been the experience of one developing nation after another: products that were once luxuries available only to a small elite soon became the daily fare of an expanding middle-class, and soon even the poor had access to a range of goods and services formerly beyond the imagination of even emperors. However, we must again remember the lesson of the "Irishman's two stoves"—continued travel in the same direction can readily reach a point where it becomes self-defeating. So it is with our culture of consumer choice. If freedom is the capacity for meaningful action, as we have said, more choices may not mean more freedom, since the mind can only meaningfully distinguish between a limited number of options.

Consider for instance Netflix or the cereal aisle at a modern supermarket. At first glance, both of these epitomize a glorious realization of the modern idea of freedom. Here we find ourselves, more than any previous generation (or indeed any previous year), "free to choose," as Friedman put it. The possibilities before us are nearly endless. But therein lies the problem. All of us are probably familiar with the experience of paralysis that can take hold in these situations and myriad others like them—a listless, restless, aimless browsing that becomes ever less satisfying the longer we look, and in the end, we pick a movie to watch or a high fructose corn syrup concoction to eat, almost at random. But of course, randomness is the opposite of purposefulness, the opposite of free action. What has happened in situations like these is that the possibilities have multiplied beyond the point where rational choice is viable, particularly given the relatively inconsequential nature of the decisions.

Faced with such paralysis, we frantically search for some form of guidance to orient our decision making, some source of meaning. This wish, too, the market is happy to grant. As most of us are now only too well aware, we are perhaps more passive than active when it comes to choosing the next title to watch on Netflix. The almighty algorithm nudges us gently but firmly toward what Netflix thinks we might most enjoy—or else, in the case of Netflix's own original content, toward what Netflix *wants* us to enjoy. Indeed, it may well be that we opened Netflix in the first place not so much as a purposeful free decision, but as the end result of a long sequence of algorithmic nudges from advertisements or social media feeds, which all conspire to tell us what we *really* want.

While the technology may be new, the basic principle is not. On the contrary, such "nudges" (a term coined by behavioral economists Richard Thaler and Cass Sunstein)[2] are ubiquitous in a market economy and not just in obvious ways like

---

[2] Richard H. Thaler and Cass R. Sunstein, *Nudge: The Final Edition* (New York: Penguin, 2021).

advertisements or celebrity endorsements. Let's consider that cereal aisle again. It may look like a random array of 200 different options, but you can guarantee that there is a method in the supermarket's madness. Some of those cereals will go on the hard-to-reach top shelf, others at eye level, and others at toddler level. Grocery stores often charge suppliers more for the privilege of putting their products in the most eye-catching locations, and makers of sugary kids' cereals have long known that they can maximize sales by putting them where the kids can most easily see them, grab them, and begin the long but inevitable campaign to wear down parental resistance.

Indeed, advertisers know well that the ideal consumer is a child, since children are quite poor at distinguishing between different kinds of desire and are unable to resist acting on impulses. But since children don't have much disposable income, adults must be conditioned to think and act like children.[3] Hence the modern market economy's constant campaign (intensified exponentially by digital technology) against one of the basic conditions of "adulting"—deferred gratification. Increasingly unable to restrain our irrational desires, or even to distinguish rational desires from irrational ones, more and more of us are entering our twenties, thirties, or even forties in an essentially childlike state of immediate impulse-gratification. Needless to say, such childishness is not conducive to the profound self-denial and

---

[3] See Benjamin Barber, *Consumed: How Markets Corrupt Children, Infantilize Adults, and Swallow Citizens Whole* (New York: W. W. Norton, 2008), chap. 1. See also W. T. Cavanaugh, *Being Consumed: Economics and Christian Desire* (Grand Rapids, MI: Eerdmans, 2008), chap. 1; and Richard Thaler, *Misbehaving: The Making of Behavioral Economics* (New York: W. W. Norton, 2015), sec. 3.

deferred gratification required by marriage and childbearing; little wonder, then, that so many developed societies are facing demographic collapse.

Since the market economy is built on the ideal of ever-increasing consumption and since there are built-in biological limits to what any human being can consume in the traditional, literal sense (i.e., food and drink), it has been the study of entrepreneurs and advertisers to blur the boundaries between needs, wants, and mere urges. By the magic of the Industrial Revolution, goods and services once seen as rare luxuries were converted into staples—a process that for a long time was seen as a vast expansion of human freedom. (I, for one, have no desire to go back to the days when indoor plumbing was a rare luxury.) But this process of increasing freedom by increasing consumption cannot go on forever.

Once we approach the frontier where all ordinary needs and wants are met, continued economic growth requires an acceleration in the rate at which products are used up, transforming formerly durable goods like furniture or clothing into consumables that we expect to replace within a few years or a few months. Electronics are often built with "planned obsolescence" in mind, as Apple or Google seeks to convince you that a perfectly functional smartphone must be discarded in favor of one with more cameras or fewer buttons. Even better than planned obsolescence is the manufacture of new wants or desires—a process that is most successful when products are geared less toward finite biological needs and more toward our seemingly boundless psychological needs. The most effective products are those that *create* more desires even as they seem to meet them, whether these be traditional addictive substances like alcohol or nicotine or the more powerful addiction machines of social media. These products offer to assuage our loneliness and depression but tend to intensify such feelings the more we use them. The result, as we have seen in the previous chapter, is not freedom but slavery: "They promise them freedom, but they themselves are slaves of corruption. For whatever overcomes a person, to that he is enslaved" (2 Pet 2:19).

The False Freedom of Productive Wealth[4]

For the biblical writers, then, it is clear that economic freedom is not found in greater and greater consumption but in a very different vision of wealth. The economic ideal of the Old Testament in particular can be summed up in the famous passage "but they shall sit every man under his vine and under his fig tree, and none shall make them afraid" (Mic 4:4; cf. 1 Kgs 4:25). The vision here is one of economic *independence* made possible by the ownership of land, which for most premodern societies functioned as the primary form of wealth. The connection between land and freedom, indeed, continued to constitute a powerful ideal right into the American Founding era. Noah Webster, for instance, a prominent advocate of the new US Constitution before he was known as the author of the *American Dictionary*, wrote, "*Property* is the basis of *power* . . . [and thus] the means of preserving our freedom. . . . A general and tolerably equal distribution of landed property is the

---

[4] For a fuller version of the argument in the sections that follow, see my "A Theology of Money," *Mere Orthodoxy* 3 (Summer 2022), https://mereorthodoxy.com/a-theology-of-money/.

whole basis of national freedom."[5] Land freed its owner from worry, want, and dependence; it freed him from being forced to serve someone else or wait on charity to get by; it freed him from being so preoccupied with material things that he had no leisure (and thus liberty) to reflect on higher things and deliberate soberly.[6] Land could do this because land was fundamental to all means of production: food above all, of course, but also the fibers that could be made into clothing, trees that could be made into wood, stone that could be used in building. In an agrarian economy, there was little of any value that you could produce without access to land; and to be landless, whatever one's wits or brawn, was to be largely at the mercy of those who did have land. Landed wealth, then, meant *self-sufficiency*, not just the freedom from want in the moment but the freedom from fear of want in the future.

Even such freedom, although far more robust than the freedom of the consumer in the candy shop, can quickly become its own form of slavery, however. Consider the rich young ruler, whose great wealth shackled him so that he lacked the freedom to follow Christ. "How difficult it is," remarks Jesus, "for those who have wealth to enter the kingdom of God! For it is easier for a camel to go through the eye of a needle than for a rich person to enter the kingdom of God" (Luke 18:24–25). Why is this? Jesus gives us further insight in his "parable of the rich fool" in Luke 12:16–21:

---

[5] Noah Webster, "Leading Principles of the Constitution," in *The American Republic*, ed. Bruch Frohnen (Carmel, IN: Liberty Fund, 2002), 293.

[6] See Hannah Arendt, *The Human Condition*, 2nd ed. (Chicago: University of Chicago Press, 1998), 58–67.

> The land of a rich man produced plentifully, and he thought to himself, "What shall I do, for I have nowhere to store my crops?" And he said, "I will do this: I will tear down my barns and build larger ones, and there I will store all my grain and my goods. And I will say to my soul, 'Soul, you have ample goods laid up for many years; relax, eat, drink, be merry.'" (Luke 12:16–19)

The most striking thing about this little soliloquy is its solipsism: "to himself," "I," "I," "my," "I," "I," "my," "I," "my," "my," "I," "my." Here is a man whose wealth has caused him to become completely *incurvatus in se* (again, curved in upon himself), so much so that he makes little speeches to himself, talking to his soul like an old friend. He has made an idol of the independence that wealth offers. "But God said to him, 'Fool! This night your soul is required of you, and the things you have prepared, whose will they be?' So is the one who lays up treasure for himself and is not rich toward God" (Luke 12:20–21).

The land that God gave to Israel in the Promised Land, after all, was meant to be not merely a means of relative independence but, at the same time, a reminder of the Israelites' radical *dependence* on God's gift. The rich fool and the rich young ruler have failed to heed the warning of Deut 8:11–14:

> Take care lest you forget the LORD your God . . . lest, when you have eaten and are full and have built good houses and live in them, and when your herds and flocks multiply and your silver and gold is multiplied and all that you have is multiplied, then your heart be lifted up, and you forget the LORD your God, who brought you out of the land of Egypt, out of the house of slavery.

If we forget that our wealth is a symbol of our dependence on the One who brought us out of slavery, our wealth will become the means of a new and worse form of slavery.[7]

Not only does the accumulation of wealth enslave its owner, it frequently involves oppression of one's neighbor. The Old Testament prophets are full of denunciations of the exploitation of the poor by the rich; indeed, the prophets seem to link the mere accumulation of land with injustice: "Woe to those who join house to house, who add field to field, until there is no more room, and you are made to dwell alone in the midst of the land" (Isa 5:8). Why is this? The biblical writers are not Marxist revolutionaries. They clearly accept the reality that wealth will be unequally distributed and, indeed, hold up many rich men as models of godliness and recipients of God's blessing. However, when the primary form of wealth is land, the pursuit of wealth is in large measure a zero-sum game. One family in Israel could increase its land only at the expense of its neighbor losing land. Hence the ideal of "every man living under his own vine and fig tree" required restraints on accumulation: at the establishment of the Promised Land, God divided up the land so that every family would have some measure of self-sufficiency, and God instituted various provisions in the law to ensure that this would remain the case. Leviticus 25 insists that "land shall not be sold in perpetuity" (v. 23). If any Israelite becomes poor and

---

[7] The following books have been particularly helpful to me in analyzing biblical teaching on wealth and poverty: David L. Baker, *Tight Fists or Open Hands?: Wealth and Poverty in Old Testament Law* (Grand Rapids, MI: Eerdmans, 2009); Craig L. Blomberg, *Christians in an Age of Wealth: A Biblical Theology of Stewardship* (Grand Rapids, MI: Zondervan, 2013); and Luke Timothy Johnson, *Sharing Possessions: What Faith Demands*, 2nd ed. (Grand Rapids, MI: Eerdmans, 2011).

was forced to sell, a relative should redeem it for him, and if that was not possible, it would still return to the original owner at the Year of Jubilee (every fifty years). Moreover, those who held land, remembering their own dependence on God, should not try to reap the full benefits of their wealth but leave the corners of their field for the landless to glean (Leviticus 19). The book of Ruth, often read by moderns as a charming biblical love story, is rather, more than anything else, a lesson in biblical economics: Boaz stands forth as an exemplar of how to use wealth faithfully rather than allowing it to become an idol.

Market Failures and the Limits of Politics

Today we like to think that we have transcended the problem of wealth as a "zero-sum game," replacing finite land with seemingly infinite money. Money can be invested in many different forms of productive capital, so it is possible to grow your own wealth by *enriching* your neighbor, rather than impoverishing him. True enough, although the replacement of land with money brings with it a host of new problems, at least land can be loved as a piece of God's good creation; but money is an incorporeal abstraction, making it far easier to idolize and far less able to serve as a source of meaning. Simone Weil writes, "Money destroys human roots wherever it is able to penetrate, by turning desire for gain into the sole motive. It easily manages to outweigh all other motives, because the effort it demands of the mind is so very much less. Nothing is *so* clear *and so* simple as a row of figures."[8]

---

[8] Simone Weil, *The Need for Roots: Prelude to a Declaration of Duties towards Mankind*, trans. Arthur Wills (New York: Routledge, 2001), 44.

Moreover, the replacement of land with money and capital is no guarantee against exploitation. In the ideal market transaction, both seller and buyer gain. But many transactions are far from ideal; they are what economists call "market failures." Such failures occur, for instance, when there is "asymmetric information"—when a buyer knows something the seller does not or (much more often) when the seller knows something the buyer does not. It is the task of law to prevent such injustices so that market participants can bargain on a fair footing; thus, for instance we have laws requiring home sellers to disclose the existence of lead paint or other hazardous materials on the property and laws prohibiting insider trading.

A more pervasive market failure results from "monopoly power": whenever one person controls access to something that many people need, that individual will be in the position to dictate terms to his or her advantage. If I manage to corner the market for silicon chips, I will be able to ratchet up the price substantially, using my wealth to impoverish rather than enrich my neighbor. Land is inherently monopolistic since there is only so much of it to go around, and those lucky enough to stake a first claim to a desirable bit of real estate can reap enormous profits when others move in. With other resources, monopoly power tends to be more elusive; but because it is so lucrative, many businesses put most of their energies in this direction: trying to buy up competitors or drive them out of businesses, applying for copyrights and patents (monopolies over intellectual property), or cornering strategic new markets before competition emerges. So we should beware of making careless contrasts between the "freedom" of the market and the "coercions" of laws and governments. "Buy this or else you'll starve" can be every bit as coercive as "don't sell this or else you'll go to jail."

Governments thus have an appropriate role in passing laws to limit the accumulation or abuse of monopoly power, but laws can also frequently strengthen monopolies, especially laws intended to prevent other forms of market failure. Consider for instance the many regulations set by the Food and Drug Administration. Most of these were intended to prevent shady producers from exploiting information asymmetries to pawn off tainted foods or snake oil drugs on unsuspecting consumers, but those regulations can also entrench monopoly power when they keep small drug producers from competing with Big Pharma or small dairy farmers from selling raw milk. Many of the regulations currently on the books are there because monopolistic businesses actively lobbied for them in order to drive smaller competitors out of business. No wonder many of us have grown so cynical of both "big business" and "big government," which seem so often to be in collusion to amass power to oppress and exploit. "Behold, the tears of the oppressed, and they had no one to comfort them! On the side of their oppressors there was power, and there was no one to comfort them" (Eccl 4:1).

Accordingly, while there is nothing wrong with trying to use good laws to create and maintain the conditions necessary for a truly free market (relative equality, information transparency, enforceable contracts, well-defined property rights, and so on), we should also be honest about the fact that political institutions on their own can do little to ensure market freedom. In a society where everyone is determined to thieve and exploit, the only way to maintain order will be through draconian and pervasive police powers; but in such a society, won't the police themselves be corrupt and take bribes? Accordingly, while much more might be said in other contexts about concrete economic policies Christians might promote, I want to close this section by emphasizing that, ultimately, a truly free market is possible only among truly free people.

Becoming Free People

It is worth noting that even while, in a modern economy, many forms of wealth may not actually *be* zero-sum, the way we *feel* about wealth is nearly always zero-sum. The rich young ruler could glory in the fact that, being far wealthier than most of his fellows, he was freed from any sense of dependence on them, and indeed knew that they often depended on him. Even if he enjoyed none of the luxuries we take for granted today, he was wealthy in the sense that matters most to fallen human beings— he could rejoice that he had far more freedom and power than his fellows, that he was master of his own life. Thus, regardless of whether it is the case that you can only *get* rich by making others poor, it is true that most of us only *feel* rich in relation to others who are poorer, which tempts us in all our economic interactions not to seek our neighbor's shared good but our own good at their expense.

Once again, then, we find that our various external forms of unfreedom have their root in deeply internal forms of unfreedom, both moral and spiritual. There is indeed nothing new under the sun, and it is remarkable that our present condition can be well summarized in terms of what Thomas Aquinas outlined 750 years ago as the two vices related to wealth: *greed* (or *covetousness*) and *prodigality*.[9] In greed, we mimic the inward

---

[9] See Thomas Aquinas, *Summa Theologiae*, trans. the Fathers of the English Domenican Province, IiaIIae, Qs. 118, 119; https://www.newadvent.org.

turning of the rich fool in the parable, retreating into ourselves and seeking to be self-sufficient. When we do this, we deny the fundamental reality of our created dependence. "Come now, you who say, 'Today or tomorrow we will go into such and such a town and spend a year there and trade and make a profit'—yet you do not know what tomorrow will bring. What is your life? For you are a mist that appears for a little time and then vanishes" (Jas 4:13–14). The first thing Scripture tells us about ourselves is that we were formed from the dust of the ground and made alive by the breath of God: we are wholly dependent, secure only as we rest upon God. The second thing the Scripture says about us is, "It is not good for man to be alone." We are never more human than when we are sharing, and in nothing is the fall clearer than in the barrier it introduces to such sharing (the first thing Adam and Eve did was hide their bodies from one another). Greed, then, is fallen man's descent into solipsism and self-love.

If in greed we lose our true selves by turning inward and cutting ourselves off in false self-sufficiency, in *prodigality*, we lose ourselves by turning outward and dissipating ourselves in a hundred vain quests to find pleasure, satisfaction, and meaning in earthly goods and experiences. The preacher in Ecclesiastes 2 describes such materialistic pursuits vividly: "I said in my heart, 'Come now, I will test you with pleasure; enjoy yourself'" (v. 1). He goes on to vividly describe his materialistic pursuits in terms not that different from our own perversions of the American Dream: a summer home with lavish landscaping and a swimming pool, service workers to spare him any drudgery, plenty of food, and of course, music and sex. Like us, he thought he deserved such pleasures because he had *worked* for them: "This was my reward from all my toil" (Eccl 2:10). But "then I considered all that my hands had done and the toil I had expended in doing it, and behold, all was vanity and a striving after wind, and there was nothing to be gained under the sun" (Eccl 2:11). While the greedy save too much, the prodigal—more common in modern America—spend too much. But both act out of idolatry. Well did Augustine write in his *Confessions*, "You have made us for yourself, O Lord, and our hearts are restless until we rest in you."[10]

This does not mean that we must, like some desert ascetic, abandon all forms of earthly wealth and spend all our time in rapturous meditation upon the divine. Indeed, the medieval monks who most consistently carried out such an unearthly ideal could do so only by depending upon the earthly labors of ordinary laypeople who raised crops with which to feed the monks and built houses for them to stay in. The things of earth are part of God's good creation, and he meant for us to enjoy them. Indeed, after dismissing such pleasures as "vanity and striving after wind," Ecclesiastes exhorts us, "Go, eat your bread with joy, and drink your wine with a merry heart, for God has already approved what you do. Let your garments be always white. Let not oil be lacking on your head. Enjoy life with the wife whom you love, all the days of your vain life that he has given you under the sun, because that is your portion in life and in your toil at which you toil under the sun" (Eccl 9:7–9). But this will only work if we "remember also [our] Creator," and "fear God and keep his commandments" (Eccl 12:1, 13).

---

[10] Augustine, *Confessions*, trans. J. G. Pilkington, in *Nicene and Post-Nicene Fathers, First Series*, ed. Philip Schaff, vol. 1 (Buffalo: Christian Literature, 1887), I.1.1, https://www.newadvent.org/fathers/110101.htm.

The right relation of the Christian to wealth is one of grateful detachment: (1) receiving all earthly goods as true gifts of God and reminders of our dependence upon him and (2) joyfully making use of them while (3) refusing to rest in them or grow too attached to them. This is what it means to be "poor in spirit" (Matt 5:3). Augustine again comes to our aid, explaining this posture of soul with his distinction between "use" and "enjoyment" and his idea of rightly ordered loves. All created things are good, but they are good in relation to their Creator; therefore, we ought to love all of them, but in the proper order—in relation to God. Properly speaking, only God himself is an object of *enjoyment*—that is, something or rather Someone in whom we take pleasure for his own sake, as an end in himself. All other goods are to be *used* in relation to this highest end, enjoyable only inasmuch as they participate in and draw us toward God.

Only by cultivating such a spiritual freedom of resting upon God can we experience the moral freedom from greed and prodigality that enables our hearts to relate rightly to wealth, that enables us to buy and sell for the good of our neighbor as well as ourselves. And only a society of people who have cultivated such detachment and who refuse to find their highest value in monetary value, their highest pleasure in what money can buy, will be able to maintain the institutions, customs, and laws that foster political liberty and authentically free markets.

7

Freedom and Faith: Getting Real about Religious Liberty

> Live as people who are free, not using your freedom
> as a cover-up for evil, but living as servants of God.
> —1 Peter 2:16

> My conscience is captive to the Word of God. I
> cannot and I will not retract anything, since it is
> neither safe nor right to go against conscience.
> I cannot do otherwise, here I stand,
> may God help me, Amen.
> —Martin Luther, The Diet of Worms (April 18, 1521)

Why Religious Liberty?

Perhaps no form of liberty is liable to get as much attention today among American Christians as *religious liberty*. As we find ourselves transformed from dominant cultural majority to an increasingly embattled minority, we cannot resist the sense that our religious liberty is under threat, even as the courts have significantly expanded religious liberty protections in recent years. This is not just our imagination—we really do find ourselves in a society increasingly intolerant of Christian orthodoxy or traditional morality. But on this subject perhaps more than any other, our modern intuitions about liberty may be apt to mislead us, and if we are not careful, we will find ourselves advancing a godless vision of personal autonomy under the noble banner of religious liberty. Here again our earlier distinctions between *negative* and *positive*, *inward* and *outward*, *individual* and *corporate* freedom can come to our aid, enabling us to think more clearly about the conditions (and limits) that make religious liberty possible.

But first we must ask why we should favor religious liberty in the first place. This question might seem downright heretical for most modern Western Christians. After all, nearly all Americans since our Founding have accepted the proposition that every individual has a natural right to religious liberty. This once meant that everyone could worship God according to his or her own convictions of how God desires to be worshipped, but it has gradually expanded to include a right to worship any god or indeed no god. Such an expansive vision of religious liberty has become one of America's chief exports to the rest of the world, enthusiastically lobbied for by American Christians seeking to end the persecution of Christians abroad.

But any sober study of history will show us that Christians throughout the centuries have not necessarily shared our fixation with religious liberty. During the spread of Christianity in Europe, it was not uncommon for whole nations to "convert" at once because their rulers accepted Christianity and immediately insisted their people do likewise—or else. The great Christian emperor Charlemagne infamously baptized thousands of Saxon captives at once by threatening them with drowning: they had to go into the water either way, but if they wanted to come out of it again, they'd better do so as Christians. During the later Middle Ages, the Catholic Church established elaborate mechanisms for hunting down and interrogating heretics, and if the accused failed to recant, they were handed over to civil magistrates for execution. The Protestant Reformers rejected such practices but still took for granted that it was a Christian ruler's responsibility to protect the church by restraining the teaching or public practice of false religion. Of course, it is impossible to appeal directly to Scripture in support of our contemporary ideal of religious freedom: Old Testament rulers were praised by God's prophets for their willingness to punish idolaters and promote the worship of Yahweh. Perhaps the New Testament changed this paradigm; but with no Christian rulers in view at the time, the text is silent on the matter. When the early church *was* blessed with its first Christian emperor, Constantine, many assumed as a matter of course that he would repress paganism by force.[1]

---

[1] Of course, in recent generations it has been common to question whether Constantine's reign was really more of a blessing than a curse for the early church. Ethicists like John Howard Yoder and Stanley Hauerwas influentially contended that "Constantinianism" represented the captivity of the church to the idolatry of worldly power. However, for a powerful and persuasive response, see Peter J. Leithart, *Defending Constantine: The Twilight of an Empire and the Dawn of Christendom* (Downers Grove, IL: IVP Academic, 2010).

It would not be hard to argue that our contemporary celebration of religious liberty is inseparable from our contemporary religious indifferentism. Perhaps it is because we don't think that religion really matters much, because most of us (even self-identified evangelicals) think there are many ways to God,[2] that we happily indulge any and all forms of religious practice and shudder at the intolerance of anyone who would say otherwise. Our ancestors, who took their faith quite seriously, could imagine no offense more grievous than to publicly blaspheme God's name or to lead another soul astray on the path to hell—surely fines, imprisonments, or exile were mild penalties in comparison to so great a crime!

We need not accept such a cynical explanation. There are certainly other, better reasons for the expansion of religious liberty than mere indifferentism, and Christians have strong grounds both theological and prudential to support a legal regime that offers generous protections and exemptions for individual conscience claims. We cannot afford to be unwary, however, of how the ideal of religious liberty has morphed into a blank check for libertinism or served as a Trojan horse within the church weakening our public witness or capacity for public action. In the wake of the *Dobbs* decision that overturned *Roe v. Wade*, some pro-abortion plaintiffs have filed suits citing that the right to abort was for them a matter of religious conviction and thus enjoyed First Amendment protection.[3] If Christians

---

[2] See for instance Joe Carter, "The State of Theology: What Evangelicals Believe in 2022," *The Gospel Coalition*, September 22, 2022, https://www.thegospelcoalition.org/article/state-theology-2022/.

[3] See for instance *Anonymous Plaintiffs 1–5, et. al v. The Individual Members of the Medical Licensing Board of Indiana*, et al., September

are to offer a strong and coherent case for religious liberty that does not degenerate into moral anarchy, we must think long and hard about what it might mean to have a *right* to believe and do what is *wrong*, and to what extent such a right deserves protection by law.

Religious Liberty in the Reformation

For Protestants, our ideal of religious liberty is liable to still be shaped by Luther's famous speech at the Diet of Worms in 1521. Hauled before the emperor to answer for his heresies, Luther could not have faced higher stakes. If unconvinced of Luther's submission to the pope and his definition of the Catholic faith, Charles V might well have handed Luther over to be burned at the stake despite Charles V's assurances of safe conduct, as had happened to Jan Hus a century earlier. It quickly became clear that the Catholic authorities were interested not in a conversation but in a recantation, demanding that Luther retract all of his writings and teachings over the past few years. After long prayer and meditation, Luther courageously refused, saying, "Unless I am convinced by the testimony of the Scriptures or by clear reason . . . I am bound by the Scriptures I have quoted and my conscience is captive to the Word of God. I cannot and will not retract anything, since it is neither safe nor right to go against conscience. May God help me. Amen."[4]

8, 2022, https://www.documentcloud.org/documents/23329379-order-on-preliminary-injunction-anonymous?responsive=1&title=1.

[4] Joshua J. Mark, "Luther's Speech at the Diet of Worms," *World History Encyclopedia*, December 9, 2021, https://www.worldhistory.org/article/1900/luthers-speech-at-the-diet-of-worms/.

Inspiring words, to be sure, without which the history of the Western world might have been very different. But exactly what do they have to teach us about religious liberty? It is striking that Luther, far from using the language of freedom, uses the language of bondage: "My conscience is *captive* to the Word of God." This is the *positive liberty* to obey, not the *negative freedom* to be left alone. As we have argued throughout this book, freedom always stands in relation to authority—you cannot be free from everything, but you can escape slavery only by accepting servitude to some new master, and the truest freedom is found, as Paul insisted, in becoming bondslaves of God. For Luther, then, the freedom of his conscience from all merely earthly authority only made sense as the flip side of his conscience's subjection to divine authority. Would such freedom still apply for the conscience that cast off the yoke of the Word of God or perverted the words of Scripture to suit its own whims, as Luther's opponents claimed he had done? Could there be a *right* to *wrong belief*?

In a certain sense, yes—or so Luther was prepared to argue in his *On Secular Authority*, written the following year. There he outlined some strikingly modern ideas of religious liberty, beginning with the claim that "where the soul is concerned, God neither can nor will allow anyone but himself to rule. And so, where secular authority takes it upon itself to legislate for the soul, it trespasses on [what belongs to] God's government, and merely seduces and ruins souls."[5] Luther's logic in defense of this claim

---

[5] Martin Luther, *On Secular Authority: How Far Does the Obedience Owed to It Extend?*, in Harro Höpfl, ed., *Luther and Calvin on Secular Authority* (Cambridge: Cambridge University Press, 1991), 23.

is straightforward: "Every authority can only act . . . where it can see, know, judge, adjudicate, and change things."[6] As we noted in chapter 1, there is a kind of inward liberty that lies beyond the reach of human rulers since they cannot see what goes on in the heart and soul. Nor do they have the power to alter the soul, at least at the deepest level (a corollary of Luther's doctrine of justification by faith): "They cannot force people to do more than obey by word and [outward] deed; they cannot compel the heart, even if they were to tear themselves apart trying."[7] This message—that it is impossible to coerce the conscience, and thus wrong even to try—became a standard mainstay of Protestant teaching and political theory. There must, in short, be religious liberty in the *inward* dimension. But what about the *outward* dimension?

In this treatise, Luther argued even for an external freedom in religious matters, anticipating the objection that "secular authority does not compel belief; it merely, by the use of outward means, prevents people from being led astray by false doctrine."[8] According to this argument, you may not be able to convert an unbeliever or a heretic by force, but you may well be able to use force to prevent him trying to convert others to his error—and why wouldn't you, when something as important as the salvation of souls is at stake? Luther, however, argues that such efforts will be counterproductive: "Neither faith nor heresy are ever stronger than when mere force, rather than the Word of God, is used against them."[9] Instead godly rulers must leave it

---

[6] Luther, 25.
[7] Luther, 26.
[8] Luther, 30.
[9] Luther, 31.

to pastors to refute false teaching by means of true teaching and persuasive reasoning.

On this broader argument, Luther was to find himself an outlier among the first few generations of Protestant leaders, and he later modified his views somewhat in response to the proliferation of radical groups who (to his mind) abused the Protestant gospel as a means to reject all Christian orthodoxy and human authority. More representative of the dominant view among the magisterial reformers was Heinrich Bullinger, leader of the Zurich reformation, who wrote, "The catholic verity teacheth that the care of religion doth especially belong to the magistrate, and that it is not in his power only, but his office and duty also to dispose and advance religion."[10] The phrase "dispose and advance" may have sounded innocuous enough, but it included coercion. Indeed Bullinger, seeing little difference between old and new covenants on this point, went on to say that "the Lord commandeth the magistrate to make trial of doctrines, and to kill those that do stubbornly teach against the scriptures, and draw the people from the true God."[11] This stance was defended on the grounds of *corporate liberty*, stressing that a community could only be free to render covenantal obedience to God inasmuch as it could enforce such obedience upon its members. Could this more medieval notion be squared with Luther's much more tolerant teaching?

---

[10] Heinrich Bullinger, *Decades* (1549), II.7, "Of the Magistrate, and Whether the Care of Religion Appertain to Him or No," in *Reformation Theology: A Reader of Primary Sources with Introductions*, ed. Bradford Littlejohn and Jonathan Roberts (Moscow, ID: Davenant, 2017), 423.

[11] Bullinger, 424.

A Classical Protestant Theory of Religious Liberty[12]

Over the century that followed, Protestants developed a reasonably coherent theory of religious liberty (albeit a rather more confused and conflicted practice of it) based on several key premises and distinctions.

First, these Protestants began with the fundamental conviction, voiced by both Paul in Romans 13 and Peter in 1 Peter 2, that it is the God-given task of civil authority *to punish evil and to praise or reward good*. Government's task is both negative and positive, even if in a world rife with sin and scarce in resources, most governments have to focus their efforts on restraining the worst forms of evildoing rather than the positive promotion of good.

But what defined "evil" and "good"? For the Reformers, the answer was generally "The natural moral law, as summed up in the Ten Commandments."[13] The Ten Commandments provided a shorthand summary of the entire moral universe, encapsulating first man's duties toward God in the First Table (commandments 1–4 in the Reformed numbering) and then man's duties toward his neighbor in the Second Table (commandments 5–10). Thus, it was the God-given task of government to restrain evil and promote virtue across the full scope of the Decalogue,

---

[12] For a fuller version of the arguments in the sections that follow, see my essay, "Against 'Religious Liberty,'" *American Reformer* (November 29, 2022), https://americanreformer.org/2022/11/against-religious-liberty/.

[13] See, for instance, Westminster Shorter Catechism, Q. 41: "The moral law is summarily comprehended in the Ten Commandments" (https://thewestminsterstandard.org/westminster-shorter-catechism/#41).

ensuring both that God was publicly honored and that temporal goods like life, property, and marriage were secured.

At first glance, then, this theory of law was all-encompassing, and there would seem to be no room for religious liberty. But Protestant thinkers limited this broad remit in a couple of ways, one traditional and another newer and radical. First, they shared with Thomas Aquinas the notion that it was the task of civil law to limit itself to goods and evils where *the common good* was at stake.[14] That is, the mere private virtues and vices of individuals were between themselves and God. Only inasmuch as these behaviors affected the good of the community as a whole did they become the concern for civil rulers. Of course, in practice such lines can be very hard to draw. Is drunkenness a private vice or a public menace? Well, it may begin as the former but can readily become the latter if left unchecked. The Ten Commandments themselves highlight the ambiguity by including a final commandment, the tenth, which is directed to the inward motions of the heart: coveting. As Luther noted, no ruler can restrain what he cannot see, and so coveting is outside the reach of human law. Yet coveting can easily spill over into theft and other forms of public vice, so perhaps it behooves the godly ruler to try at least to minimize occasions for coveting? Indeed, on precisely this basis, for centuries many Protestants supported laws limiting the sale and ostentatious display of luxury goods.

The Reformers went further than Aquinas, though, with their "two-kingdoms" distinction, grounded on the doctrine of justification by faith, which distinguished sharply between the inward man in relation to God and the outward man in relation

---

[14] Aquinas, *Summa Theologiae*, IaIIae, Q. 96, articles 1–3.

to neighbor.[15] Since no outward works in themselves could please God, there could be, as Luther had emphasized, no point in using human law to secure true obedience to and honor of God. What then was the relevance of the First Table in the new covenant? A consensus gradually emerged that although civil authorities should not enforce moral duties toward God *as such*, they could and should enforce them inasmuch as they served the temporal common good.

That is to say, idolatry has both earthly and eternal consequences. The magistrate has no concern with the latter, but the former is certainly his business. If idolatrous worship or public blasphemy harms the life of the nation—say, by undermining the reverence due to human authorities, the sanctity of oaths, or the control of licentious passions—then in principle a good ruler might seek to restrict such evils just as he might alcoholism or drug trafficking. After all, the moral universe is not a collection of isolated dos and don'ts with no effect on one another but a seamless whole: sin in one area spills over into many others. If Scripture teaches us anything, it is that justice and peace in society depend upon the right honoring of God: hold the Creator in contempt, and you will tend to devalue the lives of those who bear his image; refuse to recognize him as Giver of all good things, and you will tend to lay claim on the property he has bestowed on others; fail to keep faith with him, and you will not hold marriage vows in high regard either. The experience of the Western world over the past century bears eloquent witness

---

[15] See William J. Wright, *Martin Luther's Understanding of God's Two Kingdoms: A Response to the Challenge of Skepticism* (Grand Rapids, MI: Baker, 2010); W. Bradford Littlejohn, *The Two Kingdoms: A Guide for the Perplexed* (Moscow, ID: Davenant, 2017).

to the interweaving of the First and Second Tables of the Law. Again, civil law cannot directly ensure that anyone honors God and his gifts truly. But it can promote the work of the church, which helps work such inward renewal, and it can try to protect at least an outward public recognition of the moral Lawgiver so as to ensure an outward conformity with public morality.

Based on these principles alone, there may be liberty of *conscience*, but it does not automatically follow that there should be liberty of *worship* or *proselytizing* or *religious exercise*—three things that we now take for granted as part of a full-fledged religious liberty. Any of these things might plausibly be restrained for the sake of the common good, and some still are (we do not permit Mormons to practice polygamy or Wiccans to practice human sacrifice). However just because governments are authorized *in principle* to restrain false religion doesn't mean they *should* most of the time. This will depend entirely on the prudential question of whether the resort to coercive force will do more harm than good.

Luther was one of the first to argue that coercive force would do more harm than good when it came to matters of ultimate conviction. When people feel that the deepest core of their identity is at stake, and perhaps their eternal salvation, will they actually be restrained by fear of legal penalties, or will they simply be tempted to resort to desperate measures, measures that will tear civil society apart? Over time, Protestant rulers came more and more to the conclusion that only the most dangerous forms of false teaching and grotesque forms of corrupt religious practice should be restrained by threat of punishment. As much as possible, error should be dealt with by persuasion, as Luther had at first advised. This steady replacement of coercion with persuasion was made possible in large part by the immense expansion of education and literacy that followed the Reformation: people who are able to read and write may be reasoned out of their errors rather than merely intimidated. It also depended upon the cultivation of a *culture* of toleration. After all, it did no good for rulers to formally permit freedom of religious assembly for dissenters if angry mobs gathered to obstruct their services or torch their church buildings, as happened countless times in early modern Europe.

Toleration versus Affirmation: Religious Liberty in Crisis

Religious liberty, in other words, is a fragile achievement, not one to be taken for granted. It depends upon a distinction between ultimate and penultimate things, a recognition that, as Gandalf sagely observes in Tolkien's *The Return of the King*, "It is not our part to master all the tides of the world."[16] Our world today, in revolt against the very idea of the transcendent, sees no reason why it should not fall to humans to root out every injustice and recondition every deviant. Religious liberty depends upon a literate people committed to the goal of rational persuasion as a substitute for violence. Today, we inhabit an increasingly illiterate society in which words themselves have been recharacterized as a form of violence and in which reason is dismissed as a tool forged by the privileged for the oppression of the marginalized. Above all, religious liberty depends on the

---

[16] J. R. R. Tolkien, *The Return of the King* (New York: Houghton Mifflin, 1988), 155.

cultivation of the virtue of tolerance: on a posture of the soul (and habits of mind and speech) that manages to hold together the propositions "This matters deeply, and I am convinced this person is deeply wrong" *and* "It's not my job to set this person straight." As a society, we stopped exercising our tolerance muscles several decades ago, around the time that we decided that the idea of "tolerance" itself was a form of oppression.

After all, to speak of "tolerating" something conveys that I still think that it is bad, something whose absence would, in my view, make the world a better place. Toleration thus implies judgment and condemnation, even if the tolerant person knows how to keep that condemnation to himself. The culture of toleration once promoted by political philosophers like John Milton and John Locke has been replaced with a culture of *affirmation*, in which I do not really feel free as long as I know that I am surrounded by the disapproval of others. This development can be laid at least in part at the feet of John Stuart Mill, who, as we saw in chapter 3, argued in his famous essay "On Liberty" (1864) that freedom before the law was not enough, for the norms and expectations of civil society could be every bit as oppressive. Constricted by the stuffy Victorian morality of the world he inhabited, Mill longed to breathe freely in a society that encouraged and fostered as much freedom of thought and expression, as much individuality, as possible.

Mill, of course, took most of traditional morality for granted and never imagined that this call for unfettered individualism would find expression in delusions like the transgender movement, but his principles pointed unmistakably in that direction. Any attempt for a society to privilege or promote one set of values as intrinsically better than another, he implied, necessarily resulted in a constriction of "liberty." Thus, all viewpoints, values, and lifestyles must be equally "affirmed." But of course, as we now know well, this is impossible. Morality is too deeply inscribed on us, and we know in our bones that some things are better than others. Accordingly, it did not take long for this culture of *affirmation* to turn against toleration. In the 1960s and 1970s, our society started teaching that all religious convictions and lifestyles were equally good. By the 2010s, it had shifted, insisting that only the most progressive convictions and lifestyles should be celebrated, while traditional ones did not even deserve toleration.

Getting Real about Religious Liberty

In answer to this, we must own up to the basic facts of human nature: we cannot help but discriminate between true and false, right and wrong, and no one is a consistent relativist, able to pretend that even one's own moral values are mere subjective preferences. Accordingly, every society, every legal structure, embodies certain convictions about what evils should be shunned and what goods should be pursued. A healthy society, we may conclude, will be one that exercises humble restraint about what evils to restrain, at least when deep religious convictions are involved. But it need not follow that society should abandon every effort to distinguish between which convictions should be platformed and promoted and which should not. No society can maintain such "neutrality" for long.

Moreover, we should return to the very first principle of Protestant political thought noted above and remember that government is tasked not only with punishing evil but with praising and rewarding the good. For most of American history, despite our nation's commitment to religious liberty and formal disestablishment, Christianity has enjoyed government support in the form of tax exemptions, educational support, public prayer, and much more. A healthy culture of religious liberty can certainly coexist with—indeed, may endure for long in—a society that uses public norms and institutions to positively promote Christian faith and practice.

A final point to be made about religious liberty is that, like every form of freedom that we have considered in this book, it depends upon limits. To take it too far, assuming that there cannot be too much of a good thing, will quickly make nonsense of it. After all, if by religion we mean something like "a deeply held conviction about the Supreme Being or beings and the duties required by him/them," it will quickly become apparent that not all religious convictions can be acted upon without grave harm to others and to the fabric of society. Accordingly, whether it was Anabaptists' religious convictions that civil authority and private property were to be disregarded, Quakers' religious convictions against military service, Mormons' religious commitment to polygamy, or Christian Scientists' religious refusal to offer lifesaving blood transfusions to their children, even the most tolerant civil governments have insisted that such convictions could not be accommodated without danger to its citizens or to society as a whole. Over time, some exemptions have been carved out even for such groups, but with the recognition that their claim to religious liberty is not automatic or absolute. All the more so do we refuse freedom to religions that summon their adherents to holy war against us.

Such commonsense limitations sit uneasily with the ideal of absolute religious freedom embraced in the later twentieth century, an ideal thoughtlessly promoted today by many Christians. Even worse, though, has been the broadening definition of religion to encompass any kind of subjective, deeply held conviction, no matter how idiosyncratic or injurious to others. For instance, one reason that courts used to hesitate to grant religious exemptions to pacifists objecting to military service was that before long, non-Quakers would pretend to be Quakers just to avoid the dangers of war. Judges thus required that conscientious objectors provide proof that they actually belonged to religious groups with principled stands against war. By the Vietnam War, however, judges began to allow any individual with a deep-seated personal opposition to the war to opt out on "religious" grounds. We might like the idea of living in a society in which no one ever has to do something they don't personally support, but we should recognize this as a luxury of superpower status. If America were ever to face an existential threat, she might not be able to defend herself with an all-volunteer army.

Without an ability to draw principled boundaries around religious liberty, founded on a commitment to certain objective religious truths, we are at risk of degenerating into moral and political anarchy in which every personal conviction, opinion, or preference is wielded as a trump card against the authority of law.

Once again, then, we see that political liberty left to its own devices is self-destructive, as observed in chapter 4. Without a foundation of citizens committed to and formed in habits of moral freedom, the liberty of permissive legal structures will degenerate into mere license. However, the problem runs much deeper. For without a Christian and especially Protestant commitment to salvation by faith alone, it is difficult to see what principled foundation there could be for a culture of religious liberty. If we assume that apathy and religious indifferentism cannot sustain themselves, that man is a naturally religious being and nature abhors a vacuum, then sooner or later even the most secular societies will find themselves moved again by some kind of religious fervor. So it is today with the religion of "expressive individualism" or its close cousin, "wokeism."[17]

Every religion, ancient or modern, will offer some account of the stain of guilt that lies heavy upon humankind, some account of how this guilt may be purged by sacrifice or violence, and some account of how individuals may share in the benefits of this purgation. For nearly all religions, the salvation thus sought will be by works: only by performing the proper rituals, punishing the proper offenders, or participating in the proper practices of self-purgation can individuals or societies be made clean. Possessed of such ideas, any religiously motivated society will have great difficulty in seeing why it should extend freedom to heretics, to those who endanger its purity structure. Why not simply force them to conform so that the wrath of the gods—or the wrath of the masses—might be placated?

For Christians, and especially the heirs of Luther, the answer is obvious: enforced conformity will never please God. Only

---

[17] The term "expressive individualism" is Carl Trueman's, from *The Rise and Triumph of the Modern Self: Cultural Amnesia, Expressive Individualism, and the Road to Sexual Revolution* (Wheaton, IL: Crossway, 2020). For an incisive analysis of the theological roots of "wokeism," see Joshua Mitchell, *American Awakening: Identity Politics and Other Afflictions of Our Time* (New York: Encounter, 2020).

true faith, which lies before and beyond all works, makes any ultimate difference. And if that is so, religious coercion makes much less sense and can only be justified in limited cases for temporal, not eternal, purposes. Only within a culture founded on such spiritual freedom—a liberation from the fear of God's displeasure—is it possible to develop the moral virtues and political practices of authentic toleration. Precisely to the extent that we fall away from this gospel into a new Pelagianism of "social justice" and "affirmation" will we find ourselves increasingly unable to sustain either the culture or the legal framework that make religious liberty possible.

CONCLUSION

> For you were called to freedom, brothers. Only do not use your freedom as an opportunity for the flesh, but through love serve one another.
> —Galatians 5:13

When it comes to "freedom," many American Christians inhabit two parallel worlds of discourse. At church, in Bible studies, and in their devotional life, they learn about how "true freedom is found in Christ": how sin is the worst form of slavery and how Jesus sets them free from sin. Freedom is a feature of their inner lives, an experience of the mind or soul—and significantly, it involves committing to one path, only one Way. Yet the rest of the week, when watching the news, doing their shopping, or arguing on social media, "freedom" is found anywhere but in Christ. It is a political or economic or therapeutic slogan, a promise for liberation from the burdensome expectations or demands of other people, a promise fulfilled in fewer rules, more stuff, and more space to call their own. Freedom is a feature of their outer lives, something experienced within the world, and something that avoids commitment and demands the maximation of options and choices.

For many of us, I think, these two different ideas of freedom travel merrily along their parallel tracks without touching. We barely pause to think about how differently we use the word in different contexts, just as we do not think twice about referring to both insects and software glitches as "bugs."

Many of us, though, make some attempt to bring the two discourses together, either adjusting our notions of spiritual freedom to conform to our worldly notions of political freedom or seeking to sacralize political freedom with spiritual significance. The former tendency appears in the rise of antinomianism among American Christians: the idea that to be "set free in Christ" is to be liberated from laws and moral expectations, that "Jesus loves us just the way we are" and we shouldn't feel any pressure to change. It can be seen in an even more extreme form in the "prosperity gospel," which encourages Christians to think of their spiritual liberation in Christ as a ticket to worldly freedom, understood in the crassest terms as the multiplication of their buying power.

The latter can be seen in the tendency of many American Christians to endow America itself with spiritual significance as the unique vehicle of God's purposes in the world. From within this understanding, American ideals of political freedom come to be seen as something much greater and nobler than merely the improvement of democratic institutions—the Constitution becomes rather a kind of Fifth Gospel by which God announces his purposes to save the kingdoms of the world by bringing them under the sway of American liberty. Such idolatrous visions have been part of the American imagination almost since the beginning of our nation, and they have become only more dangerous as hope in America has dimmed. Fearful that the nation on which they have staked so much of their sense of purpose will fail to achieve its promise, some American Christians seem ready to stake everything on one last throw to try to "make America Christian again" by any means necessary.

We may be quick enough to see the errors in these conflations of sacred and secular visions of liberty, but these visions testify to our instinctive longing to reintegrate these two divided halves of our souls. Freedom is not merely a spiritual reality or a worldly ideal; it is not merely inward or outward. Freedom, rather, is experienced above all in the conformity of the soul to reality, the fit between our wills and our world, that moment when everything clicks into place and we find ourselves able to be and to do what it is we feel *meant* to be and to do. The freedom of the skilled violinist to express the melodies welling up within her on a perfectly tuned instrument, the freedom of the seasoned alpine skier with acres of white powder spread out below him, the freedom of a great orator with a life-or-death argument to make and an audience hanging on her every word—each of these describes an experience in which inner life and outer life have been brought into alignment, in which the soul itself has been finely tuned as an instrument to carry out a sense of vocation, and in which the world offers itself as a fit vehicle for those purposes because they conform to the norms God has built into creation.

As we have seen in this book, however, and as we experience every day of our lives, this ideal alignment of purposes with possibilities can be broken in any number of ways. We may find ourselves with a clear sense of purpose but frustrated by circumstances, like the budding young musician whose family cannot afford an instrument or lessons. Or we may find ourselves with the world at our feet but at the mercy of our desires—like a billionaire playboy who could have anything he wants but who cannot see beyond the next bottle of alcohol or the next sexual escapade.

Nor can we recover freedom simply by aligning inward desires with outward conditions. For our inner lives themselves are complex and conflicted. Our desires are at war with one another and at war with our Creator. "Unite my heart to fear your name" (Ps 86:11), prays the psalmist, recognizing that the greatest threat to piety is plurality—the inability to bring the conflicted fragments of his soul together in obedience to God. Behind and beyond all these warring desires lurk the shadowy fears of failure, inadequacy, and judgment, the worry that even if I could get my act together and accomplish something for once, someone would be standing over my shoulder saying, "Not good enough," or that someone else would come along and reduce it to rubble. "It is an unhappy business that God has given to the children of man to be busy with. I have seen everything that is done under the sun, and behold, all is vanity and a striving after wind" (Eccl 1:13–14).

Freedom therefore must start at the innermost heart of our being, as we saw in chapter 2, as we hear the word of love and the promise that sets us free from fear, futility, and forgetfulness and that makes us, in the words of the Heidelberg Catechism, "wholeheartedly willing and ready from now on to live for him." From there, we begin the arduous lifelong task of "keep[ing] in step with the spirit" (Gal 5:25) as he unites our hearts to fear God's name, enabling us to take every thought and desire captive to the obedience of Christ (2 Cor 10:5), as we saw in chapter 3. This newfound freedom is not a freedom to "find yourself" or "be yourself," as the world tells us, but a freedom *for* the neighbor. Or rather, it is the freedom that comes from finding oneself *in the neighbor*: "For you were called to freedom, brothers. Only do not use your freedom as an opportunity for the flesh, but through love serve one another. For the whole law is fulfilled in one word: 'You shall love your neighbor as yourself'" (Gal 5:13–14). We are enabled to most truly be ourselves within the body of Christ; our individual freedom is experienced within a community.

This should not surprise us if freedom is, as we defined it in chapter 1, "the capacity for meaningful action." If my actions are to have meaning, there must be a community within which they make sense, a community that understands what I am trying to communicate. As a teacher, I've often had the experience of dealing with frustrated students who come to me toward the end of the term and share that they don't understand key concepts or that they disagree with things I am teaching. "But there was time every class for free discussion or Q&A. Why didn't you pipe up sooner?" I always ask, even though I know the answer by now. It is very hard to speak up if you feel like you're the only one who doesn't get it or that your insights or perspectives might not be welcome (and odds are you will feel that way even if it isn't true). Each of us longs for a community, a context, where we understand one another and feel understood by one another; there at last we are free to express ourselves, to contribute something. The best classical musician in the world will still need an orchestra from time to time.

This explains much of the rise of "identity politics." Thrown into a world in which nothing seems given anymore and everything seems up for grabs, we gravitate desperately toward communities of belonging within which we can make sense of our desires, purposes, and vocations. There is nothing wrong with this *per se*; the problem comes when I demand that these communities simply "affirm me the way I am," even if I am a bit out of touch with reality—as all of us, warped by sin, are to some extent. When we do this, we find ourselves creating entire communities that are disconnected from reality, communities organized around the sole purpose of making their members *feel* free, whatever the painful truth may be. If freedom demands a fit between the soul and the world, what do we do when our souls are at war with the world as God made it and we do not want to change? Well, we construct a world of our own within which we can experience a kind of faux freedom: a family, a tribe, a sexual identity-group, a political party. Within each of these social worlds, a shared sense of meaning is possible that offers its members a sense of freedom, but often this internal consistency is achieved only at the cost of collective delusion, a blindness to the fine-grained contours of reality.

Modernity, however, holds out the promises that perhaps we need no longer conform the soul to reality, our wills to the world: we can instead conform reality to the shape of our own wills, as we saw in chapter 5. "We built our own world," boasts the protagonist in Christopher Nolan's masterpiece *Inception*, speaking for modern man in a technological age. By means of technology, we dream, we can overcome the sense of dislocation between ourselves and our surroundings, redrafting the blueprint of creation, rewriting even our own DNA, as the latest biotechnology promises. We hope to experience the freedom of the divine nature, infinitely creative and all-powerful, speaking new worlds into being.

This longing discloses the truth that we were indeed meant to experience the freedom of the divine nature—but not in the way the world whispers to us, echoing the lie of the serpent: "Your eyes shall be opened, and ye shall be as gods" (Gen 3:5 KJV). We have a harder road to walk, following in the way of our Savior:

> His divine power has granted to us all things that pertain to life and godliness, through the knowledge of him who called us to his own glory and excellence, by which he has granted to us his precious and very great promises, so that through them you may become partakers of the divine nature, having escaped from the corruption that is in the world because of sinful desire. (2 Pet 1:3–4)

Our culture tells us that there is corruption in the world because of *other people*, because of capitalism or socialism or "the patriarchy" or feminism; that these forces outside of us interfere with the freedom that is our birthright. But Scripture tells us that corruption is in the world because of sinful desire—*our* sinful desire. We can be transformed only by the renewal of our minds, by which we learn not to give free rein to our will but to "discern what is the will of God, what is good and acceptable and perfect" (Rom 12:2). Within that will, we find our own wills anew, buried as they had been under a mountain of sin. Within that will also we find a new community of belonging, the church, a space within which we can be ourselves by learning to deny ourselves, and within which we are not merely affirmed in who we were but are challenged to become who we were meant to be.

Thus called to freedom and equipped by Christ, his Word, and his people to stand firm in that freedom, we will be enabled to take that freedom out into the world, reordering our political communities, our markets, and our technologies to discern and serve God's creative purposes—and pointing each of these creaturely goods toward that final freedom of souls washed clean in a world made new around the throne of God.

SELECTED BIBLIOGRAPHY

Note: In addition to the sources cited in this book, I have listed other key titles that have been seminal in my previous thinking and writing on this book's subject.

Adams, John. *Novanglus* (1774–75). In *The Political Writings of John Adams*. Edited by George W. Carey. Washington, DC: Regnery, 2000.

Althusius, Johannes. *Politica Methodice Digesta* (1603). Reprinted as *The Politics of Johannes Althusius*. Translated and edited by Frederick S. Carney. London: Eyre and Spottiswoode, 1965.

Aquinas, Thomas. *Summa Theologiae*. Translated by the Fathers of the English Dominican Province. At New Advent, https://www.newadvent.org.

Arendt, Hannah. *Between Past and Future*. Introduction by Jerome Kohn. New York: Penguin, 2006.

———. *The Human Condition*. 2nd ed. Introduction by Margaret Canovan. Chicago: University of Chicago Press, 1998.

Aristotle. *Nicomachean Ethics*. Translated by W. D. Ross. In *The Basic Works of Aristotle*. Edited by Richard McKeon. New York: Modern Library, 2001.

———. *Politics*. 2nd ed. Translated by Carnes Lord. Chicago: University of Chicago Press, 2013.

Augustine, *Confessions*. Translated by J. G. Pilkington. In *Nicene and Post-Nicene Fathers, First Series*. Edited by Philip Schaff. Vol. 1. Buffalo, NY: Christian Literature, 1887. https://www.newadvent.org/fathers/110101.htm.

Austin, Victor. *Up with Authority: Why We Need Authority to Flourish as Human Beings*. Edinburgh: T&T Clark, 2010.

Avis, P. D. L. *The Church in the Theology of the Reformers*. Atlanta: John Knox, 1981.

Baker, David L. *Tight Fists or Open Hands?: Wealth and Poverty in Old Testament Law*. Grand Rapids, MI: Eerdmans, 2009.

Barber, Benjamin. *Consumed: How Markets Corrupt Children, Infantilize Adults, and Swallow Citizens Whole*. New York: W. W. Norton, 2008.

Bauckham, Richard. *God and the Crisis of Freedom: Biblical and Contemporary Perspectives*. Louisville: Westminster John Knox, 2002.

Berlin, Isaiah. "Two Concepts of Liberty." In *Liberty: Incorporating Four Essays on Liberty*. Edited by Henry Hardy. Oxford: Oxford University Press, 2002.

Biggar, Nigel. *What's Wrong with Rights?* Oxford: Oxford University Press, 2020.

Blomberg, Craig L. *Christians in an Age of Wealth: A Biblical Theology of Stewardship*. Grand Rapids, MI: Zondervan, 2013.

Boethius. *The Consolation of Philosophy*. Translated by V. E. Watts. London: The Folio Society, 1998.

Burke, Edmund. *Reflections on the Revolution in France and Other Writings*. Edited by Jesse Norman. Everyman's Library. New York: Alfred A. Knopf, 2015.

Calvin, John. *Institutes of the Christian Religion*. 2 vols. Edited by John T. McNeill. Translated by Ford Lewis Battles. Louisville: Westminster John Knox, 1960.

Carter, Joe. "The State of Theology: What Evangelicals Believe in 2022." *The Gospel Coalition*. September 22, 2022. https://www.thegospelcoalition.org/article/state-theology-2022/.

Cavanaugh, William T. *Being Consumed: Economics and Christian Desire*. Grand Rapids, MI: Eerdmans, 2008.

Cicero. *On the Good Life*. Edited by Michael Grant. New York: Penguin, 1971.

Cooper, Kody W., and Justin Buckley Dyer. *The Classical and Christian Origins of American Politics: Political Theology, Natural Law, and the American Founding*. Cambridge: Cambridge University Press, 2022.

Cranz, F. Edward. *An Essay on the Development of Luther's Thought on Justice, Law and Society*. Cambridge, MA: Harvard University Press, 1959.

Deneen, Patrick J. *Why Liberalism Failed*. New Haven: Yale University Press, 2018.

Dreisbach, Daniel L. *Reading the Bible with the Founding Fathers*. Oxford: Oxford University Press, 2017.

Dunnington, Kent. *Addiction and Virtue: Beyond the Models of Disease and Choice*. Downers Grove, IL: IVP Academic, 2011.

Epictetus. *The Golden Sayings of Epictetus*. Translated by Hastings Crossley. Harvard Classics. Vol. 2. New York: P. F. Collier and Sons, 1937.

Fortescue, John. *On the Laws and Governance of England*. Edited by Shelley Lockwood. Cambridge Texts in the History of Political Thought. Cambridge: Cambridge University Press, 1997.

Friedman, Milton, and Rose Friedman. *Free to Choose: A Personal Statement*. New York: Harcourt Brace Jovanovich, 1980.

Frohnen, Bruce, ed. *The American Republic: Primary Sources*. Indianapolis: Liberty Fund, 2002.

Grant, George. *Technology and Justice*. Toronto: Anansi, 1986.

Hall, Mark David. *Proclaim Liberty Throughout All the Land: How Christianity Advanced Freedom and Equality for All Americans*. New York: Post Hill, 2023.

Hawley, Josh. *The Tyranny of Big Tech*. Washington, DC: Regnery, 2021.

Hayek, F. A. *The Road to Serfdom: Text and Documents*. Edited by Bruce Caldwell. Chicago: University of Chicago Press, 2007.

Hazony, Yoram. *Conservatism: A Rediscovery*. New York: Regnery, 2022.

———. *The Virtue of Nationalism*. New York: Basic Books, 2018.

Hill, W. Speed, and Georges Edelen, eds. *The Folger Library Edition of the Works of Richard Hooker*. Vol. 1: *The Laws of Ecclesiastical Polity: Pref., Books I–IV*. Cambridge, MA: Belknap Press of Harvard University Press, 1977.

———. *The Folger Library Edition of the Works of Richard Hooker*. Vol. 2: *The Laws of Ecclesiastical Polity: Book V*. Cambridge, MA: Belknap Press of Harvard University Press, 1977.

Hill, W. Speed, and P. G. Stanwood, eds. *The Folger Library Edition of the Works of Richard Hooker*. Vol. 3: *The Laws of*

Ecclesiastical Polity: Books VI, VII, VIII. Cambridge, MA: Belknap Press of Harvard University Press, 1981.

Hobbes, Thomas. *Leviathan*. Edited by C. B. Macpherson. New York: Penguin, 1985.

Höpfl, Harro, ed. *Luther and Calvin on Secular Authority*. Cambridge: Cambridge University Press, 1991.

James, Samuel D. *Digital Liturgies: Rediscovering Christian Wisdom in an Online Age*. Wheaton, IL: Crossway, 2023.

Jefferson, Thomas. *Jefferson: Political Writings*. Edited by Joyce Appleby and Terence Ball. Cambridge: Cambridge University Press, 1999.

Johnson, Luke Timothy. *Sharing Possessions: What Faith Demands*. 2nd ed. Grand Rapids, MI: Eerdmans, 2011.

Johnston, Henry P., ed. *The Correspondence and Public Papers of John Jay*. 4 vols. New York: Burt Franklin, 1970. First published 1890.

Kahneman, Daniel. *Thinking, Fast and Slow*. New York: Farrar, Straus and Giroux, 2013.

Kant, Immanuel. *Groundwork to the Metaphysics of Morals*. Translated and edited by Mary Gregor and Jens Timmermann. Cambridge: Cambridge University Press, 1998.

———. "What is Enlightenment?" (1784). *Modern History Sourcebook*. https://sourcebooks.fordham.edu/mod/kant-what is.asp.

Kidd, Thomas. *God of Liberty: A Religious History of the American Revolution*. New York: Basic Books, 2012.

Leeman, Jonathan. *Political Church: The Local Assembly as Embassy of Christ's Rule*. Downers Grove, IL: IVP Academic, 2016.

Leithart, Peter J. *Defending Constantine: The Twilight of an Empire and the Dawn of Christendom*. Downer's Grove, IL: IVP Academic, 2010.

Lewis, C. S. *The Abolition of Man*. New York: Macmillan, 1960.

———. *The Great Divorce*. New York: HarperCollins, 2001.

———. *The Screwtape Letters*. New York: HarperCollins, 2001.

Littlejohn, Bradford. "Against 'Religious Liberty'." *American Reformer*. November 29, 2022. https://americanreformer.org/2022/11/against-religious-liberty/.

———. "Individual and National Freedom: Towards a New Conservative Fusion." *American Affairs* (August 2020). https://americanaffairsjournal.org/2020/08/individual-and-national-freedom-toward-a-new-conservative-fusion/.

———. *The Peril and Promise of Christian Liberty: Richard Hooker, the Puritans, and Protestant Political Theology*. Grand Rapids, MI: Eerdmans, 2017.

———. "A Theology of Money." *Mere Orthodoxy* 3 (Summer 2022). https://mereorthodoxy.com/a-theology-of-money/.

———. *The Two Kingdoms: A Guide for the Perplexed*. Moscow, ID: Davenant Press, 2017.

———, Bradley Belschner, and Brian Marr, eds. *Hooker's Laws in Modern English*. Vol. 1: *Preface–Book IV*. Moscow, ID: Davenant Press, 2019.

———, and Jonathan Roberts, eds. *Reformation Theology: A Reader of Primary Sources with Introductions*. Moscow, ID: Davenant Press, 2017.

Locke, John. *Political Writings*. Edited by David Wootton. Indianapolis: Hackett, 2003.

Luther, Martin. *The Freedom of a Christian*. In *Three Treatises*. 2nd rev. ed. Translated by W. A. Lambert. Revised by Harold J. Grimm. Philadelphia: Fortress, 1970.

———. *Martin Luther's 95 Theses, with Introduction, Commentary, and Study Guide*. Edited and translated by Timothy J. Wengert. Minneapolis: Fortress, 2015.

———. *Preface to the Letter of St. Paul to the Romans*. Translated by Andrew Thornton. Christian Classics Ethereal Library. https://www.ccel.org/l/luther/romans/pref_romans.html.

Mark, Joshua J. "Luther's Speech at the Diet of Worms." *World History Encyclopedia*. December 9, 2021. https://www.worldhistory.org/article/1900/luthers-speech-at-the-diet-of-worms/.

Medaille, John C. *Toward a Truly Free Market: A Distributist Perspective on the Role of Government, Taxes, Health Care, Deficits, and More*. Wilmington, DE: ISI Books, 2010.

Mill, J. S. "On Liberty." In *On Liberty, Utilitarianism, and Other Essays*. Edited by Mark Philp and Frederick Rosen. Oxford: Oxford University Press, 2015.

Mitchell, Joshua. *American Awakening: Identity Politics and Other Afflictions of Our Time*. New York: Encounter, 2020.

Montesquieu, *The Spirit of the Laws*. Edited by Anne Cohler, Basia Miller, and Harold Stone. Cambridge Texts in the History of Political Thought. Cambridge: Cambridge University Press, 1989.

O'Donovan, Oliver. *Begotten or Made?: A New Edition for the 21st Century*. Landrum, SC: Davenant, 2022.

———. *Bonds of Imperfection: Christian Politics, Past and Present*. Grand Rapids, MI: Eerdmans, 2004.

———. *The Desire of the Nations: Rediscovering the Roots of Political Theology*. Cambridge: Cambridge University Press, 1996.

———. "The Language of Rights and Conceptual History." *Journal of Religious Ethics* 37, no. 2 (2009): 193–207.

———. *Resurrection and Moral Order: An Outline for Evangelical Ethics*. 2nd ed. Grand Rapids, MI: Eerdmans, 1994.

———. *The Ways of Judgment*. Grand Rapids, MI: Eerdmans, 2005.

———, and Joan Lockwood O'Donovan, eds. *From Irenaeus to Grotius: A Sourcebook in Christian Political Thought, 100–1625*. Grand Rapids, MI: Eerdmans, 1999.

Peterson, Jordan. *Beyond Order: 12 More Rules for Life*. New York: Portfolio/Penguin, 2021.

Plato. *Five Dialogues: Euthyphro, Apology, Crito, Meno, Phaedo*. 2nd ed. Translated by G. M. A. Grube. Revised by John M. Cooper. Indianapolis: Hackett, 2002.

———. *Republic*. Translated by C. D. C. Reeve. Indianapolis: Hackett, 2004.

Pufendorf, Samuel. *The Whole Duty of Man and the Citizen According to the Law of Nature*. Edited by Ian Hunter and David Saunders. Natural Law and Enlightenment Classics. Indianapolis: Liberty Fund, 2003.

Schindler, D. C. *Freedom from Reality: The Diabolical Character of Modern Liberty*. Notre Dame, IN: University of Notre Dame Press, 2017

Schull, Natasha Dow. *Addiction by Design: Machine Gambling in Las Vegas*. Princeton: Princeton University Press, 2012.

Shain, Barry Alan. *The Myth of American Individualism: The Protestant Origins of American Political Thought*. Princeton: Princeton University Press, 1994.

Skinner, Quentin. *Liberty Before Liberalism*. Cambridge: Cambridge University Press, 1998.

Strassler, Robert B. ed. *The Landmark Thucydides: A Comprehensive Guide to The Peloponnesian War.* New York: Touchstone, 1998.

Thaler, Richard H. *Misbehaving: The Making of Behavioral Economics.* New York: W. W. Norton, 2015.

———, and Cass R. Sunstein. *Nudge: The Final Edition.* New York: Penguin, 2021.

Thompson, W. D. J. Cargill. "The 'Two Kingdoms' and the 'Two Regiments': Some Problems of Luther's *Zwei-Reiche-Lehre.*" *The Journal of Theological Studies* 20, no. 1 (1969): 164–85.

Tierney, Brian. *Liberty and Law: The Idea of Permissive Natural Law, 1100–1800.* Washington, DC: Catholic University of America Press, 2014.

Tolkien, J. R. R. *The Return of the King.* New York: Houghton Mifflin, 1988.

Trueman, Carl R. *The Rise and Triumph of the Modern Self: Cultural Amnesia, Expressive Individualism, and the Road to Sexual Revolution.* Wheaton, IL: Crossway, 2020.

Ursinus, Zacharias. *The Heidelberg Catechism.* https://www.rca.org/about/theology/creeds-and-confessions/the-heidelberg-catechism/.

Verkamp, Bernard. *The Indifferent Mean: Adiaphorism in the English Reformation to 1554.* Athens, OH: Ohio University Press, 1977.

Walker, Andrew T. *Liberty for All: Defending Everyone's Religious Freedom in a Pluralistic Age.* Grand Rapids, MI: Brazos, 2021.

Weil, Simone. *The Need for Roots: Prelude to a Declaration of Duties towards Mankind.* Translated by Arthur Wills. New York: Routledge, 2001.

Wilson, James. *Lectures on Law*. In *Collected Works of James Wilson*. Edited by Kermit L. Hall and Mark David Hall. 2 vols. Indianapolis: Liberty Fund, 2007.

Witte, John E., Jr. *Law and Protestantism: The Legal Teachings of the Lutheran Reformation*. Cambridge: Cambridge University Press, 2002.

———. *The Reformation of Rights: Law, Religion, and Human Rights in Early Modern Calvinism*. Cambridge: Cambridge University Press, 2007.

Wright, William J. *Martin Luther's Understanding of God's Two Kingdoms: A Response to the Challenge of Skepticism*. Grand Rapids, MI: Baker Academic, 2010.

Zuboff, Shoshana. *The Age of Surveillance Capitalism: The Fight for a Human Future at the New Frontier of Power*. New York: PublicAffairs, 2019.

SUBJECT INDEX

A

Abolition of Man, The (Lewis), 46, 56, 89, 93–94, 96, 98
abortion, 10, 13, 15, 59, 98, 128
acedia, 91. *See also* Nothing, the
action, meaningful, 8, 17, 22, 37, 67, 109, 149
Act of Toleration, 72
Adam, 5, 86, 95, 121
Adams, John, 79, 82
Adams, Samuel, 82
addiction, 49, 93–94, 112–13. *See also* bondage
affirmation, 137–39, 143
Age of Surveillance Capitalism, The (Zuboff), 94
Alcoholics Anonymous, 29
alienation, 22, 91
Alito, Samuel, 15

America
and freedom, 64
and the free market, 106–7
and public morality, 74
American Christians, 109, 125–26, 145–47
American Civil War, 7
American Dictionary (Webster), 113–14
American Dream, 121
American politics, 106
American Revolution; American Revolutionaries, 7, 12–13, 78
Anabaptists, 140
anarchism, 34, 39–40
anarchy, 35, 82, 129, 141
antinomianism, 31–32, 34, 39–40, 146
Apple (company), 112
Aquinas. *See* Thomas Aquinas

Arendt, Hannah, 67–68
Aristotle, 41, 50, 55, 60
atheists, 72
Augustine, 30, 53, 66, 84, 105, 122–23
authenticity, 57–60
authority
    divine, 34, 130
    human, 34–38, 130, 132, 135
    political, 79, 82–83, 133, 135, 140
    secular, 130–31

B

Bauckham, Richard, 3
Bed of Procrustes, The (Taleb), 85
Berlin, Isaiah, 9–10
Berlin Wall, 106
Bezalel, 87
Bible, 40, 108, 145
biblicism, 39–40
Big Data, 96
Big Pharma, 119
biotechnology, 89, 97, 150
Boaz, 117
Boethius, 52, 58, 69
bondage, 2–6, 14, 16–19, 22, 25–27, 29, 31, 41, 44–45, 49, 53–55, 59, 70, 77, 88, 101, 104, 130. *See also* chapter 6, "Freedom and the Market" (105–23)
    the roots of modern, 60–62
    to mammon, escaping the, 105–23
Book of Common Prayer, The, 43
Brexit, 12–13
Britain, 12–13, 79
Bullinger, Heinrich, 132

C

Cain (son of Adam), 87
Calvin, John, 33, 36–37, 41
capitalism, 76, 108, 151
Catholic Church, 127
Catholicism; Catholics, 40, 44, 72–73, 129, 132
Charlemagne, 127
Charles V, 129
choice, 2, 7, 10, 13, 67, 76–77, 103, 109–10, 146
Christ. *See* Jesus Christ
Christianity; Christians, 3–4, 6, 9, 12, 18–19, 24–26, 28, 30–34, 36–41, 45–47, 52, 55, 58, 61, 66, 68–70, 77, 79, 83–84, 101–3, 108–9, 119, 123, 125–28, 132, 140–42, 145–47
Christian Scientists, 140
church (the body of Christ), 3, 127
Cicero, 50–51, 55
Commentary to the Heidelberg Catechism (Ursinus), 46

communism, 108
community, 8, 11–14, 16, 18, 36, 61, 67, 69–70, 77, 81, 95, 132, 134, 149, 151
condemnation, 21, 26, 29–30, 138
Confessions (Augustine), 105, 122
conscience, 30, 33–34, 36–40, 47, 61, 71, 82–84, 125, 128–31, 136
consent, 79–84
Consolation of Philosophy, The (Boethius), 52, 69
Constantine, 127
Constantinianism, 127
Constitution, US, 113, 146
consumer, 5, 76, 95, 102, 106–7, 114, 119
consumerism, 12, 108–13
consumption, 112–13
courage, 12, 48, 50. *See also* virtue
COVID-19 pandemic, 8, 12, 38
Cranmer, Thomas, 43
creation, 2, 58, 85–89, 104, 117, 122, 147, 150
Creator, 64, 86–88, 122–23, 135, 148

D

David (king of Israel), 84, 87
Decalogue, 133. *See also* Ten Commandments

Declaration of Independence, the (Jefferson), 64, 79
deliverance. *See chapter 2, "The Great Deliverance"* (21–41)
Democratic Party, 106–7
depression, 23–24, 26–27, 113
Desire of the Nations, The (O'Donovan), 54
Diet of Worms, The (Luther), 125, 129
Diogenes the Cynic, 51
Dobbs v. Jackson Women's Health Organization (2022), 13, 128
Dreisbach, Daniel, 83

E

Eden, 5, 96
Egypt, 3, 115
England, 72, 74
Enlightenment, 60
Epictetus, 51, 55
eudaimonia, 64
EU (European Union), 12–13
Europe, 71, 126, 137
European Union. *See* EU
evangelicalism; evangelicals, 34, 36, 40, 128
Eve, 5, 86, 90, 95, 121

F

faith, 25–27, 30–31, 39, 54, 62, 105. *See chapter*

7, "Freedom and Faith" (125–43)
fear, 19, 21–25, 32, 44, 50, 80, 83, 103, 114, 148
First Table, 133, 135–36. *See also* Ten Commandments
Food and Drug Administration (US), 119
forgetfulness, 21–24, 28–30, 32, 148
forgiveness, 31, 44, 54
Founders, American, 62, 67, 73, 77, 79, 82, 113, 126
freedom. *See chapter 1, "What Is Freedom?"* (1–20); *see also* liberty
   economic, 7, 19. *See chapter 6, "Freedom and the Market"* (105–23)
   and faith. *See chapter 7, "Freedom and Faith"* (125–43)
   individual, 13, 19, 60, 69, 71, 149. *See also* liberty: individual and corporate
   and the market. *See chapter 6, "Freedom and the Market"* (105–23)
   moral, 18–19, 22, 29–34, 41, 65, 80, 83–84, 104, 123, 141. *See also chapter 3, "Walking by the Spirit"* (43–62)
   distinguishing spiritual freedom from, 30–34
   political, 19, 22, 34–41, 123, 146. *See chapter 4, "Between Right and Rights"* (63–84)
   and the pursuit of happiness, 64–67
   religious. *See* liberty: religious
   sexual, 58
   spiritual, 18–19, 44–46, 53–54, 62, 80, 83–84, 104, 123, 143, 146. *See also chapter 2, "The Great Deliverance"* (21–41)
   distinguishing from moral freedom, 30–34
   and technology. *See chapter 5, "Freedom and Technology"* (85–104)
Freedom of a Christian, The (Luther), 4, 24, 31, 33, 70
free market. *See* market
Free to Choose (Friedman), 76
Friedman, Milton, 76, 106, 108–9
futility, 21–24, 26–28, 32, 80, 148

G

Gandalf, 137

Germany, 96
Google, 96, 112
government, 10, 64–67
Great Depression, 7
Great Divorce, The (Lewis), 55
Great Recession, 7
greed, 109, 120–23

H

happiness, 51–52, 56, 58, 64–67, 69, 74, 76–77
Hayek, Friedrich, 7–8, 108
health, 27, 99–100
healthcare, 99–100
Heidelberg Catechism, 21, 44, 54, 148
Henry, Patrick, 7, 63
Holy Spirit, walking by the. See chapter 3, "Walking by the Spirit" (43–62)
Homer, 48
Hooker, Richard, 35–36, 40
Hus, Jan, 129

I

idolatry, 69, 84, 122, 127, 135
"I Have a Dream" (King), 7
Iliad (Homer), 48
image-bearer, 8, 85
Inception (film), 90, 150
individuality, 7, 57, 75–76, 138
Industrial Revolution, 109, 112
Instagram, 57, 93

Institutes of the Christian Religion, The (Calvin), 33
internet, the, 72, 92, 94–95
intolerance, 73, 126, 128. *See also* tolerance
"Invictus" (poem), 16
Irishman, 88–90, 109
Israel; Israelites, 3–4, 63, 115–16

J

James (apostle), 56, 61
Jay, John, 63
Jefferson, Thomas, 65–67, 72, 74
Jesus Christ, 1–3, 6, 16–18, 21–22, 24–30, 32, 40–41, 44, 46–47, 53–54, 56, 114, 145–46, 148–49, 152
Judah (tribe), 87
justice, 48–49, 79, 97, 135, 143. *See also* virtue
justification, 22, 27–28, 30, 32–33, 44–45, 54, 131, 134–35

K

Kant, Immanuel, 51–52
Kennedy, Anthony, 15
King, Martin Luther, Jr., 6–7

L

land, 113–18. *See also* property

law, 2–3, 5, 7, 12–13, 18, 25, 29, 31–36, 39–40, 45–46, 49, 51, 54, 60–62, 64, 67, 69–72, 74–75, 77–82, 107, 116, 118–19, 123, 129, 133–36, 138, 141, 146, 149
legalism, 30, 32, 39–40
Lent, 37–38
Letter Concerning Toleration (Locke), 72
Lewis, C. S., 4–5, 46, 55–56, 89–94, 96–98, 100–101
liberalism, 65, 71–77
liberation, 3, 25, 28–29, 91, 94, 96, 143, 145–46
libertinism; libertines, 40, 57, 60, 76, 128
liberty. *See also* freedom
 individual and corporate, 9, 11–14, 18–19, 36, 72, 78, 107, 126, 132
 inward and outward, 9, 14–18, 26, 56, 126, 131, 147
 negative and positive, 9–11, 18–19, 67, 107, 126, 130
 religious, 12, 19, 66, 71. *See also chapter 7, "Freedom and Faith"* (125–43)
license, 17–18, 141
Locke, John, 72–75, 138
Luddite, 88

Luther, Martin, 4, 6, 23–34, 37, 39, 41, 43–45, 53, 70, 84, 125, 129–32, 134–36, 142

M

mammon, 105. *See in general chapter 6, "Freedom and the Market"* (105–23)
Mandela, Nelson, 16
market. *See chapter 6, "Freedom and the Market"* (105–23)
 failure, 117–20. *See also* power: monopoly
 free, 2, 8, 19, 95, 106–9, 119–20, 123
mask, 8, 38
mastectomy, 99
mastery. *See also* self-mastery
medicine, 88, 98–100
Melanchthon, Philipp, 41
Merchant of Venice, The (Shakespeare), 105
Meta (Facebook), 96
Middle Ages, 127
Mill, John Stuart, 7, 74–76, 138
Milton, John, 138
modernity, 5, 150
money, 96, 102, 105, 117–18, 123
monopoly. *See* power: monopoly
morality, 40, 58, 74, 76, 96, 126, 136, 138–39

Subject Index

Mormons, 136, 140
mortification, 46, 54

N

neighbor, 32, 38, 40–41, 65–66, 116–18, 120, 123
Netflix, 109–10
new covenant, 132, 135
New Jerusalem, 87
New Testament, 40–41, 127
Nicomachean Ethics (Aristotle), 41, 50
Ninety-Five Theses (Luther), 44
Nolan, Christopher, 150
Notes on the State of Virginia (Jefferson), 65
Nothing, the, 90–93
nudge, 110

O

Obama, Barack, 7
O'Donovan, Oliver, 8–9, 54, 100
Old Testament, 28, 40–41, 113, 116, 127
"On Liberty," 7, 74, 138
On Secular Authority (Luther), 130
Otis, James, 78–79

P

paganism; pagans, 41, 47–52, 55–56, 127
pandemic. *See* COVID-19 pandemic
Parliament (UK), 79
patience, 86, 102
Paul (apostle), 1–4, 6, 16–17, 20, 24–25, 27, 30–32, 37, 40, 43, 45, 47, 50, 53, 83, 130, 133
Pelagianism, 30–31, 143
Peloponnesian War, 68
Pericles, 68
Peter (apostle), 45, 59–60, 83, 133
Pharisaism, 30
Planned Parenthood v. Casey, 15
Plato, 43, 47–50, 53, 55–56, 58, 60
polis, 68–69, 77
pope, 34, 129
pornography, 59, 92–93, 103
poverty, 107–8, 116
power, 4–6, 15–16, 22–23, 29, 35, 49–50, 65, 70, 77–79, 86, 90, 92, 94, 96, 100, 103, 113, 118–20, 127, 131–32, 146, 151
  monopoly, 118–19
Princess Bride, The (film), 1
privacy, 95–96
prodigality, 120–23
Promised Land, 115–16
property, 10, 72, 113–15, 118–19, 134–35, 140. *See also* land

Protestantism; Protestants, 18, 30–31, 34, 40–41, 46, 66, 70–73, 127, 129, 131–34, 136, 139, 142

Q

Quakers, 140–41

R

Reagan, Ronald, 10, 76, 106
redemption, 28
Reformation; Reformers, 4, 18, 30–31, 37, 39–40, 44, 54, 66, 70–72, 127, 129, 133–34, 137
relativism, 31, 139
religious liberty. *See chapter 7, "Freedom and Faith"* (125–43)
Renaissance, 72
repentance, 29
Republican Party, 106–7
Republic, The (Plato), 43, 60
Return of the King, The (Tolkien), 137
rights, 2, 10, 15, 119. *See chapter 4, "Between Right and Rights"* (63–84)
Rights of the British Colonies Asserted and Proved, The (Otis), 78–79
Rise and Triumph of the Modern Self, The (Trueman), 58, 60

Roe v. Wade (1973), 15, 128
Roosevelt, Franklin Delano, 7, 107
Rousseau, Jean-Jacques, 60
Rowling, J. K., 17
Russia, 12–13, 96

S

salvation, 6, 28, 30–32, 37, 39, 41, 84, 131, 136, 142
sanctification, 27–28, 32, 45, 54
Saul (king), 84
Screwtape Letters, The (Lewis), 91
Scripture, 3, 22, 24, 34–36, 39–40, 45, 71, 84, 87, 108, 121, 127, 129–30, 135, 151. *See also* Word of God
Second Table, 133, 136. *See also* Ten Commandments
Second Treatise on Civil Government (Locke), 72
self-control, 50, 57
self-expression, 57–58, 76
self-government, 2, 67, 77, 82–83
self-mastery, 19, 47–54, 104
  the pagan search for, 47–52
self-sufficiency, 50, 52, 56, 114, 116, 121
Seneca, 41

Subject Index

serpent, 46, 86, 151
servant, 4, 6, 31, 45, 62, 88, 125
service, 2–3, 6, 43, 66, 69–70, 87, 107
sexuality, 58–59
sexual revolution, 59, 76
Shakespeare, William, 105
Shelley, Percy Bysshe, 58
Silas (companion of Paul), 16, 24
Silicon Valley, 97
sin, 2–3, 16–17, 19–20, 22–31, 39, 41, 44–46, 53–55, 88, 95, 133, 135, 145, 150–51
slaves; slavery, 1–7, 14, 18–20, 22, 24, 26, 43–44, 49–51, 55, 59–62, 69, 74, 80–81, 84–85, 89–90, 95, 100–101, 106, 113–16, 130, 145
smartphone, 4, 89, 92, 102–3, 112
socialism, 94, 108, 151
social media, 57, 93, 102, 110, 113, 145
sola Scriptura, 39
solipsism, 115, 121
Solomon (king), 87
soul, 14, 16–17, 21, 23, 26–27, 30, 48–53, 55–57, 61, 66, 70–71, 92, 97, 100–101, 103, 115, 123, 128, 130–31, 138, 145, 147–48, 150, 152
Soviet Union, 106
Spirit (the Holy Spirit). *See chapter 3, "Walking by the Spirit"* (43–62)
Stoics, 50–51, 56
Sunstein, Cass, 110

T

Taleb, Nassim Nicholas, 85
technology. *See chapter 5, "Freedom and Technology"* (85–104)
temperance, 50. *See also* virtue
Ten Commandments, 133–34
Thaler, Richard, 110
That Hideous Strength (Lewis), 98
Thirty-Nine Articles, 39
Thomas Aquinas, 120, 134
TikTok, 57, 60, 102
tolerance, 138–39
toleration, 72–73, 137–39, 143
Toleration Act (1689), 72
Tolkien, J. R. R., 137
Trueman, Carl, 58, 60–62
12 Step Program (Alcoholics Anonymous), 29
"Two Concepts of Liberty" (Berlin), 9
tyranny, 74, 81
tyrant, 24, 49

U

Ukraine, 12–13
unfreedom, 8, 17, 103–4, 106, 108, 120. *See also* freedom
United States Constitution, 113, 146
Ursinus, Zacharias, 46

V

Victorianism, 75
Vietnam War, 141
virtue, 41, 47–48, 50, 53–55, 64, 72, 74, 78, 102, 133–34, 138, 143

W

Washington, DC, 97
wealth, 17, 113–18, 120, 122–23
Webster, Noah, 113
Weil, Simone, 117
West, the, 19, 96, 106, 130, 135
Wiccans, 136
Wilde, Oscar, 76
Word of God, 71, 83, 125, 129–31
works (good deeds), 25, 30–31, 54, 135, 142–43
works-righteousness, 6, 39
World War II, 106

Y

Yahweh, 127
Year of Jubilee, 117

Z

Zuboff, Shoshana, 94

SCRIPTURE INDEX

Genesis
2:18 *11*
3 *86–87, 90*
3:5 *151*
3:6 *5*
3:16 *88*
3:17 *88*
3:19 *88*
4:21–22 *87*
11 *86*
11:4 *85–86*
11:6 *86*

Exodus
31:2–5 *87*

Leviticus
19 *117*
25 *116*
25:23 *116*

Deuteronomy
8:11–14 *115*

Judges
21:25 *63*

1 Kings
4:25 *113*
18:21 *25*

Psalms
86:11 *148*

Ecclesiastes
1:13–14 *148*
2 *121*
2:1 *121*
2:10 *121*
2:11 *122*
4:1 *119*

9:7–9 *122*
12:1 *122*
12:13 *122*

Isaiah
5:8 *116*

Micah
4:4 *113*

Matthew
5:3 *123*
6:33 *xv*
10:28 *25*

Luke
12:16–19 *115*
12:16–21 *114*
12:20–21 *115*
18:24–25 *114*

Acts
16:25–28 *16*

Romans
1 *50*
2:14–15 *47*
5–8 *1*
6:1 *31*
6:7 *2*
6:18 *2–3*
6:23 *25*
7 *27, 45*
7:15 *6*
7:18–19 *45*
7:19 *18*
7:22–23 *46*
7:24 *1*
8 *27*
8:1 *21, 26*
8:2 *2*
8:21 *2, 20*
8:35 *27*
8:37 *27*
12:2 *20, 151*
13 *70, 83, 133*
13:3 *83*
13:4 *83*
13:8–10 *83*

1 Corinthians
6:12 *40*
7:22 *3*
8 *37*
10:23 *40*

2 Corinthians
3:17 *20, 54*
5:15 *53*
10:5 *148*

Galatians
3:10 *25*
4:7 *4*
5 *25, 32, 45*
5:1 *1, 6*
5:4 *25*
5:13 *45, 145*

5:13–14 *32, 149*
5:16 *20*
5:16–17 *45*
5:25 *19, 148*

Ephesians
4:22 *46*
6:6 *3*

Philippians
2:7 *4*
2:13 *54*

1 Timothy
6:10 *105*

Hebrews
2:15 *24*

James
1:25 *61*
2:14–26 *32*
4:13–14 *56, 121*

1 Peter
2 *83, 133*
2:16 *45, 125*

2 Peter
1:3–4 *151*
2:17–19 *60*
2:19 *43, 113*

Revelation
21 *87*